Grandmother's

Garden Quilt

Eleanor Burns

and

Patricia Knoechel

For Mother and Father

First printing January, 1999

Published by Quilt in a Day®, Inc.
1955 Diamond St, San Marcos, CA 92069

ISBN 0-922705-97-6

Art Director Merritt Voigtlander
Production Assistant Robin Green

Table of Contents

Introduction

My sister Patricia and I grew up with flowers nurtured by our mother, Erma Knoechel. Those flowers signified the seasons of our lives. In late winter, when there was still a light dusting of snow at our Pennsylvania home, Mother cut forsythia from our hillside, and brought them inside to bloom for her Easter Egg tree. The crocus, tulips, and daffodils soon popped their heads out of the ground. Every May Day, we gathered jack-in-the-pulpit, buttercups, and stars. One Mother's Day, we gave Mother a dogwood bush to match the fragrant lilacs and beautiful purple iris by the swing. Petunias, sweet peas, and portulaca in brilliant colors thrived by the wall. Pink old fashioned roses went to the Mother and Daughter Banquet with us. In the fall, Mother sent us off to school with zinnias and chrysanthemums, carefully wrapped in wax paper. Now, Mother's favorites are cosmos and lavatera, probably because of their beautiful rose color.

Our father, Erwin Knoechel, has been gardening since his retirement. Now he has his own spots in the yard where he plants his favorite clematis, salvia, and fuchsia. He decided perennials are the best approach to gardening. On our last visit, he surprised us with an entire yard of hardy pansies.

Patty and I grew up loving flowers and sewing together. But now our schedules have us approach our crafts differently. Pat works out of her home, with a husband who cooks, cleans, does laundry, and allows her to sew as much as she wants, as long as she doesn't interfere with his woodworking.

Eleanor, Erma, and Patricia

Erwin

I, on the other hand, am the breadwinner, chief cook, entertainer, and party planner for a large extended family. I grab my moments to sew early in the morning!

So that's why we have given you a choice on your flowers – my flat and fast way, or Pat's fussy and dimensional way. So choose between one or the other, depending on your kind of lifestyle, or mix them up if you choose!

May inspiration for your fabric flowers came from the vibrant colors of the garden.

Eleanor Burns

Florence LaGanke Harris

Florence LaGanke was a quilt pattern designer whose work was syndicated nationwide under the title of the "Nancy Page Quilt Club." Each week, Florence printed one pattern from a quilt, and gave the readers a week to complete the block. A fascinating serial story about Nancy and her friends typical of the times ran along with the pattern. The "Club" was copyrighted by Publisher's Syndicate and appeared in such newspapers as the *Nashville Banner*, *Indianapolis Star*, *Dayton Daily News*, *Buffalo Times*, and the *Semi-Weekly Farm News* (Dallas, Texas). Contributions for the patterns were sent from readers in all parts of the country.

Grandmother's Garden Quilt, a series quilt, was copyrighted by the Publishers Syndicate in 1928 and 1929. The quilt is made up of seventeen flowers appliqued in pieced baskets. The original patterns, cut from the *Salt Lake Tribune*, were a gift from Joyce Yenny of Dulzura, California. The quilt maker had carefully cut and stored the patterns in a scrap book.

The original 1928 and 1929 copyrights on *Grandmother's Garden Quilt* ended their first terms in 1956 and 1957, and were not renewed for a second 28-year term. The previously copyrighted subject matter then passed into public domain.

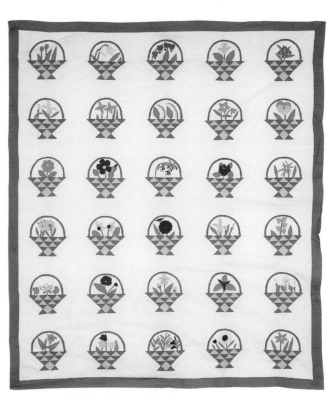

Hand quilting by Jayne Bowman

This Grandmother's Garden Quilt with border variation was made by Anna Irene Cheesebrough. Born in Wisconsin, Anna was the youngest child of Polish immigrants. After she was married, Anna lived in Long Beach, California, with her husband and four children. When her children were grown, she and her long time friend Katie Jones began getting together each week to work on quilts. They continued creating these beautiful hand pieced and quilted memories for many years. Examples of her work can be found in the homes of her children to this day. This quilt was passed on to her granddaughter, Beverly Petraglia, of Encinitas, California.

Another popular series quilt, *Garden Bouquet*, ran from February through July of 1932 in the *Nashville Banner*. Each week, Nancy printed a flower pattern in a quaint looking urn with a pair of charming birds. Nancy described the daffodil as "that spring flower which heartens all of us who are tired of the winter. My heart with rapture thrills and dances with the daffodils!"

When Nancy Page ran the "Magic Vine Quilt" in a Denver newspaper, Anne Staley Maloney carefully selected her flower fabrics at the Denver Dry Goods Company, and finished several rows. Unfortunately, she wasn't able to complete the quilt. Noel Leary of San Diego, California, was fortunate enough to inherit Anne's "ongoing" project.

Nancy writes that she got the idea for the *Magic Vine Quilt* from Jack and his magic bean vine and the fact that her own little daughter was growing just like that vine and the flowers. "Why not make a Magic Vine quilt to dream under?" she wondered.

"A downy gentian, a bouncing bet, a wild rose, a morning glory, and an evening primrose might be the friendliest of companions in the vine family. Here is a snowy white quilt with four trailing vines up and down its length. And on each vine are flowers of pleasing hue, soft pastel colors that would make the quilt a fitting covering for the cherished four poster or the modern headless and footless affair called a bed!"

Nancy Page
1930

Nancy Page Club

(The following is text copied directly from the first page of the series quilt, copyrighted by Publisher's Syndicate in 1928.)

It was the Nancy Page Neighborhood club which started it. They had been studying early American home life. They had traced the development of the architecture, the furnishings, furniture and silver. They had read of the struggles for food: and then, as things eased for these early settlers they found accounts of feasts– the kind which were served at quilting bees.

This lead them to a study of the handiwork of the early American women. References were made again and again to quilts. They saw some pictures of intricately pieced patterns and examples of wonderful quilting. A visit to the city's historical museum with its marvelous exhibit of quilts led them to rummaging in their own attics, and that, in turn, was the beginning of the famous Grandmother's Garden quilt.

"Why couldn't we make a quilt, too? We could take the flowers which grew in the old-time garden, heartsease, crocus, bleeding heart, tulip, fuchsia, bluebells and roses. We could make each block different. Think how lovely it would be. The white background, buff baskets and flowers in lavenders, blues, pinks, yellows with green for stems and leaves. Each one of us could piece one block and each block would be different. What do you think?"

Nancy had scarcely put her idea into words before the room was agog.

"Let's start right away."

"I want to piece the daffodils. I have the loveliest yellow gingham left over from Pam's dress."

"Will you design the blocks, Nancy?"

"Shall we make it for a single or double bed?"

Nancy's response was quick and willing.

"I'll try to work out patterns. Let's see how many of us are there? That will decide the number of blocks, don't you think?"

There were eighteen members of the club. As they measured the bed it looked as if twenty blocks would be needed. Should they call in two new members?

"I have it," said Nancy. "In grandmother's garden there was a rosebush at each corner. One was yellow, one was apricot, one was deep rose and one was bluish pink. Why couldn't we have a rose at each corner of the quilt?"

Nancy was elected to work out the scheme and to tell them how much material was needed. They decided to sell the quilt at the community bazaar, although each one was just as sure as could be that she would piece not only the one block for the community quilt but a whole quilt for herself. Each member was visualizing that beautiful white quilt with its drift of pastel colors in her own guest room.

They agree to come to the next meeting with scissors, needle, thimble and thread. Nancy volunteered to have the amount of material figured, to give them the size of the pieces for the basket part of the blocks, and to suggest color schemes.

Nancy was all business and figures when the quilt club came. There would be plenty of time later to gossip and drink tea. *Copyright 1928, 1929 Publishers Syndicate*

Selecting Your Fabrics

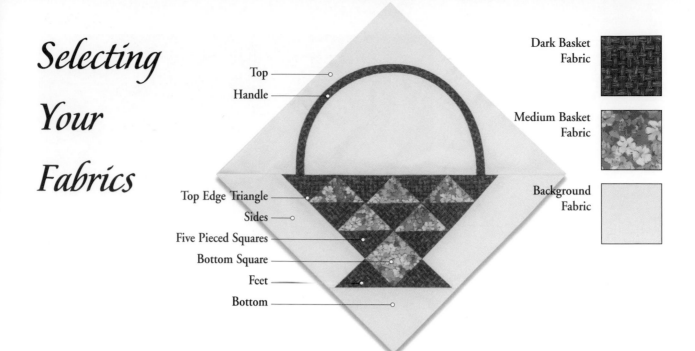

Top

Handle

Dark Basket Fabric

Medium Basket Fabric

Top Edge Triangle

Sides

Five Pieced Squares

Bottom Square

Feet

Bottom

Background Fabric

Dark Basket Fabric

Select a neutral or natural basket color or a dusty rose, blue, or lavender in a basket weave print or similar texture as Quilter's Suede. For a traditional look, select a solid. It should not be so dark or so bright that it detracts from the intensity of the flowers.

As the main fabric of the Basket, it becomes a Handle, one half of the Pieced Squares, Top Edge Triangles, and Feet. This same fabric is also used in the Sawtooth Border for the Solid Square setting and Binding.

Medium Basket Fabric

Select a small scale print, or over-all texture that's lighter than the dark Basket fabric. Avoid strong contrast in color or pattern. Florals from stripes can be used if the pattern is 3" wide.

This fabric should compliment the dark Basket fabric, as it becomes the other half of the Pieced Squares, and the Bottom Square. For a traditional look, select the same fabric as the Background.

Background Basket Fabric

Select a white or off-white textured print or solid. A dark background as medium to dark blue is also very effective. This fabric makes up the major part of the Basket in the Top, Sides, and Bottom.

Baskets shown feature fabric from the Benartex Anniversary Florals Line, designed by Eleanor Burns. Yardage requirements for Basket fabrics are on pages 16–19.

Yardage Requirements for Flower and Leaf Fabrics

Choose a variety of vibrant colors from each color family. You may follow our color suggestions and match actual fabrics as shown in the color boxes. All names and numbers refer to Benartex fabrics. Fat eighths and quarter yard cuts are perfect for this quilt.

From each color family, designate a light, medium, and dark, all closely related in value, with subtle textures, solids, or small prints. Select several large scale prints for fussy cuts. The following fabrics are enough to make up to twenty-five blocks for a king size quilt. If you vary the colors designated in the instructions, you may need more of a certain fabric.

Peach

Use for…

- Tiger Lily
- Rose

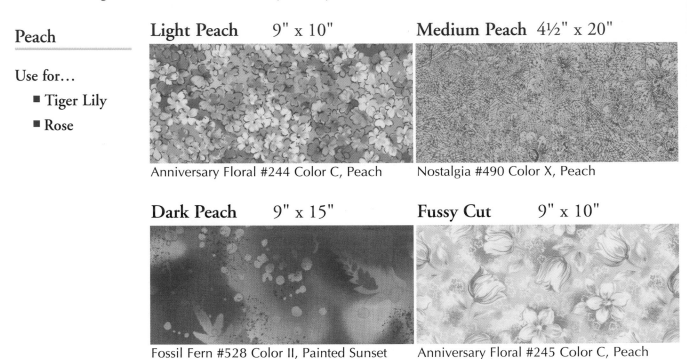

Light Peach 9" x 10"	Medium Peach 4½" x 20"
Anniversary Floral #244 Color C, Peach	Nostalgia #490 Color X, Peach
Dark Peach 9" x 15"	Fussy Cut 9" x 10"
Fossil Fern #528 Color II, Painted Sunset	Anniversary Floral #245 Color C, Peach

Purple*

Use for…

- **Morning Glory**
- **Crocus**
- **Zinnia (cut first)**
- **Canterbury Bells**
- **Pansy**
- **Fuchsia**
- **Tulip**

* Select violets with a red cast.

Light Purple 9" x 20"	Medium Purple 9" x 20"
Anniversary Floral #244 Color D, Lilac	Quilter's Suede #402 Color #60, Purple
Dark Purple 9" x 40"	Very Dark Purple 9" x 20"
Nostalgia #490 Color O, Grape	Reflections #395 Color #04, Deep Purple

Red

Use for...

- Fuchsia
- Tulip
- Shooting Star
- Rose
- Pansy
- Morning Glory
- Poppy

Fuchsia   18" x 20"

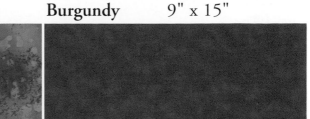

Fossil Fern #528 Color #5, Fuchsia

Burgundy   9" x 15"

Quilter's Suede #402 Color #87, Burgundy Wine

Dark Red   9" x 15"

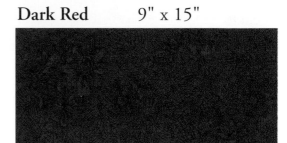

Nostalgia #490 Color Q, Raspberry

Green

Use for...

- All flowers

Light Green   9" x 20"

Fossil Fern #528 Color #30, Sage Brush

Medium Dark Green 18" x 40"

Ombre #248 Color D, Olive

Medium Dark Green 18" x 40"

Ombre #248 Color F, Green

Dark Green   9" x 15"

Reflections #395 Color AA, Forest Moss

Fussy Cut   9" x 20"

Everglade #530 Color C, Sage

Pink

Use for...

- Rose
- Trillium
- Bleeding Heart
- Poppy

Light Pink   9" x 10"

Quilter's Suede #402 Color #41, Petal Pink

Light Pink   9" x 15"

Nostalgia #490 Color Z, Pink

Medium Pink   9" x 20"

Anniversary Floral #244 Color A, Pink

Dark Pink   9" x 15"

Quilter's Suede #402 Color #21, Burgundy

Fussy Cut   9" x 10"

Anniversary Floral #245 Color A, Pink

Blue

Use for...

- Harebell
- Canterbury Bells
- Bluet

Light Blue   4½" x 10"

Anniversary Floral #245 Color B, Blue

Medium Blue   4½" x 15"

Nostalgia #490 Color E, True Blue

Dark Blue   9" x 15"

Nostalgia #490 Color Y, Dark Blue

Yellow

Use for...

- ■ Tulip
- ■ Rose
- ■ Jonquil
- ■ Pansy
- ■ Shooting Star

Light Yellow   9" x 20"

Wheat #120 Color N, Yellow

Medium Yellow   9" x 20"

Delicate Vines #454 Color #39, Maize

Dark Yellow   9" x 15"

Nostalgia #490 Color M, Smoky Gold

Fussy Cut   9" x 10"

Anniversary Floral #243 Color C, Yellow/Blue

Lavender *

Use for...

- ■ Canterbury Bells
- ■ Harebell
- ■ Zinnia (cut first)
- ■ Japanese Balloon Flower
- ■ Pansy

Medium Lavender 9" x 20"

Nostalgia #490 Color W, Lilac

Dark Lavender   9" x 20"

Antique Floral #3101 Color #61, Violet

* Select violets with a blue cast.

Hand Stitching
#5 Pearl Cotton or Embroidery Floss

#3 Pearl Cotton

Green

Variegated Yellow

Purple

Orange

Gold

Light Yellow

Red

Black

Pink

Green

Solid Square Setting

This is the first of two multiple size quilt settings to choose from. It looks very traditional and attractive with extensive quilting in the solid squares. In this setting, the Twin size quilt is very large. If you are making a quilt for a small Twin bed, you may choose to make only 12 blocks.

Dimensional Flowers

Queen Size by Patricia Knoechel

Solid Square Fabric

This fabric includes the Solid Squares, Side and Corner Triangles, First Border, half of the Sawtooth Border, and the Second Border.

For a traditional look, choose the same fabric as the Background in your Basket for the Solid Square. You may also choose the same fabric as the medium Basket fabric, or a fabric in the same color family as the Basket. Avoid a busy fabric, or one with high contrast. It should not overpower the Basket and Flowers, or quilting stitches.

Yardage for a One Block Wallhanging is on page 191.

Quilt Sizes	Baby	Lap	Twin	Double	Queen	King
	54" x 54" 4 Blocks	54" x 70" 6 Blocks	70" x 105" 15 Blocks	88" x 105" 20 Blocks	88" x 105" 20 Blocks	105" x 105" 25 Blocks
Basket						
Background	⅞ yd	⅞ yd	2¼ yds	2¾ yds	2¾ yds	3¼ yds
Medium	⅓ yd	⅓ yd	⅝ yd	¾ yd	¾ yd	¾ yd
Dark (Including Sawtooth)	1½ yds	1½ yds	2¼ yds	2¾ yds	2¾ yds	2¾ yds
Setting						
Solid Square Fabric (Including Sawtooth and Borders)	2½ yds	3½ yds	5 yds	6 yds	6 yds	7 yds
Finishing						
Binding 3" strips	⅝ yd (6) strips	⅔ yd (7) strips	⅞ yd (9) strips	1 yd (10) strips	1 yd (10) strips	1 yd (11) strips
Backing	3¼ yds	3¼ yds	6 yds	9 yds	9 yds	9¾ yds
Batting	58" square	58" x 74"	75" x 110"	92" x 110"	92" x 110"	110" square

Lattice and Cornerstones Setting

This is the second of two settings for multiple size quilts. It looks very attractive with a striped fabric as the Lattice, and a Cornerstone fabric that contrasts in color and texture. This layout can easily be quilted by stitching in the ditch along the lattice.

Flat Flowers

Queen Size by Eleanor Burns

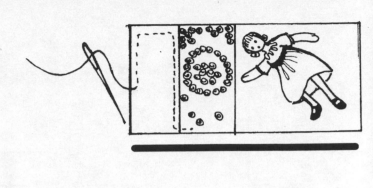

THREADBENDERS UNITE

If you are a:

stitcher	art clothing maker
quilter	dyer, batiker
basketmaker	fabric printer
embroiderer	needlepointer
knitter	beader
	doll maker

YOU SHOULD KNOW ABOUT

peninsula

stitchery

guild **PSG**

EIN: 94-3131577

FOR INFORMATION CALL: Angela Bonomo 408-725-1507

SEE OTHER SIDE

peninsula
stitchery
guild **PSG**

OFFERS YOU:

newsletters   workshops
roster   field trips
lectures   member exhibits
small working groups
communication with other fiber artists

Send to: Angela Bonomo
540 Bevans Drive
San Jose, CA 95129

NAME _____

ADDRESS _____

_____

PHONE _____ EMAIL _____

AREA OF INTEREST _____

ENCLOSE 1 YEAR MEMBERSHIP FEE $20.00

If you choose a stripe, select one with a stripe width of approximately 3", and ¼" seams on each side. Look for one with multiple repeats. Striped fabric is cut with the grain lengthwise. After the blocks are made, cut each piece ⅛" larger than block size, or approximately 12⅝" long.

Number of lattice needed for your size quilt	÷	Number of usable stripes in your fabric	=	Number of selvage to selvage strips needed	× **12⅝**	=	**Yardage Nee**ded

If you choose a Lattice other than a stripe, select a fabric in a medium to dark that appears solid from a distance so it does not detract from the Baskets and Flowers. Yardage for One Block Wallhanging on page 191.

Quilt Sizes	Baby	Lap	Twin	Double	Queen	King
	58" square	58" x 78"	70" x 110"	90" x 110"	90" x 110"	110" x 110"
	5 blocks	8 blocks	11 blocks	18 blocks	18 blocks	25 blocks
Basket						
Background	⅞ yd	1⅓ yd	1½ yds	2¼ yds	2¼ yds	3½ yds
Medium	⅓ yd	½ yd	½ yd	¾ yd	¾ yd	¾ yd
Dark	1 yd	1 yd	1⅛ yds	1¾ yds	1¾ yds	2 yds
Setting						
Striped Lattice	16 pieces	24 pieces	32 pieces	48 pieces	48 pieces	64 pieces
or						
Non-Stripe Lattice	⅔ yds	1 yd	1¼ yds	1¾ yds	1¾ yds	2⅓ yds
Cornerstones	¼ yd	¼ yd	¼ yd	⅜ yd	⅜ yd	½ yd
Side Triangles	1¼ yds	1½ yds	1½ yds	2 yds	2 yds	2 yds
Finish						
First Border 3½" strips	¾ yd (6) strips	¾ yd (6) strips	⅞ yd (7) strips	1 yd (9) strips	1 yd (9) strips	1⅛ yds (10) strips
Second Border 4½" strips	⅞ yd (6) strips	1 yd (7) strips	1⅛ yds (8) strips	1¼ yds (9) strips	1¼ yds (9) strips	1⅜ yd (10) strips
Third Border 6" strips			1¾ yds (9) strips	1¾ yds (10) strips	1¾ yds (10) strips	2 yds (11) strips
Binding 3" strips	⅔ yd (7) strips	¾ yd (8) strips	1 yd (9) strips	1⅛ yd (11) strips	1⅛ yd (11) strips	1⅛ yd (12) strips
Backing	3¾ yds	5 yds	6½ yds	9½ yds	9½ yds	9½ yds
Batting	62" square	62" x 82"	74" x 114"	94" x 114"	94" x 114"	114" square

General Cutting Instructions

6" x 6"

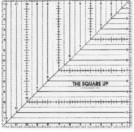

12½ " Square Up

6" x 12"

6" x 24"

Gridded Cutting Mat

Rotary Cutter

Cutting Strips and Squares

1. Make a nick on selvage edge, and tear fabric from selvage to selvage to put fabric on the straight of grain.

2. Fold fabric in half, matching torn straight edge thread to thread.

3. With fold of fabric at bottom, line up torn edge of fabric on gridded cutting mat with left edge extended slightly to left of zero. Reverse this procedure if you are left-handed.

4. Line up 6" x 24" ruler on zero. Spread fingers of your left hand to hold ruler firmly. With rotary cutter in your right hand, begin cutting at edge of fabric. Put all your strength into the rotary cutter as you cut away from you, and trim torn ragged edge.

5. **Cutting strips:** Lift and move ruler until it lines up with designated strip width on grid and cut.

6. **Cutting squares:** Place folded strip on grid. Square off left selvage edges.

7. Place Square Up ruler on strip with #1 in upper right hand corner. Place designated squaring line on cut edge. Layer cut. Square can be cut on center fold if strip is straight.

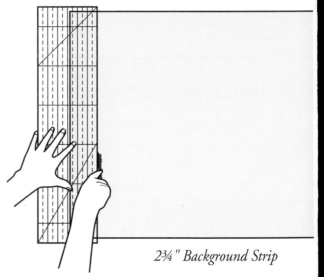

2¾ " Background Strip

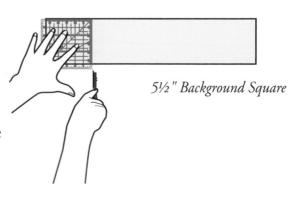

5½ " Background Square

Cutting Background Fabric

Handle Piece: Cut 13¼" strips into 13¼" squares with 16" Square Up ruler. You need one square for every two Basket blocks.

	Solid Square Setting			Lattice and Cornerstone Setting		
	13¼" Strips	into	13¼" Squares	13¼" Strips	into	13¼" Squares
Baby	1		2	1		3
Lap	1		3	2		4
Twin	3		8	2		6
Double	4		10	3		9
Queen	4		10	3		9
King	5		13	5		13

Sides: Cut 2¾" strips into 2¾" x 10" pieces. You need two pieces for every Basket block.

	Solid Square Setting			Lattice and Cornerstone Setting		
	2¾" Strips	into	2¾" x 10" Pieces	2¾" Strips	into	2¾" x 10" Pieces
Baby	2		8	3		10
Lap	3		12	4		16
Twin	8		30	6		22
Double	10		40	9		36
Queen	10		40	9		36
King	13		50	13		50

Bottom: Cut 5½" strips into 5½" squares with your 6" square ruler.
You need one square for every two Baskets.

	Solid Square Setting			Lattice and Cornerstone Setting		
	5½" Strips	into	5½" Squares	5½" Strips	into	5½" Squares
Baby			2	1		3
Lap	1		3	1		4
Twin	2		8	1		6
Double	2		10	2		9
Queen	2		10	2		9
King	2		13	2		13

Cutting Medium Basket Fabric

Pieced Squares: Cut 9" strips into 9" x 12" pieces. Each piece is enough for four Baskets plus 4 extra ◪.

	Solid Square Setting		Lattice and Cornerstone Setting	
	9" Strips	into 9" x 12" Pieces	9" Strips	into 9" x 12" Pieces
Baby		1	1	2
Lap	1	2	1	2
Twin	2	4	1	3
Double	2	5	2	5
Queen	2	5	2	5
King	2	6	2	6

Bottom Square: Cut 2½" squares from 2½" strips or left-over medium side pieces. You need one piece for every Basket.

	Solid Square Setting		Lattice and Cornerstone Setting	
	2½" Strips	into 2½" Squares	2½" Strips	into 2½" Squares
Baby		4		5
Lap	1	6	1	8
Twin	1	15	1	11
Double	2	20	2	18
Queen	2	20	2	18
King	2	25	2	25

Cutting Dark Basket Fabric

Handles: Cut one 13½" selvage to selvage strip for quilt sizes Baby to Twin. Cut two 13½" strips for Double, Queen, and King.

1. Line up the 45º line on the 6" x 24" ruler with the left selvage edge of 13½" strip.

2. Cut on diagonal. (Fabric to left of cut can be used for other parts of quilt.)

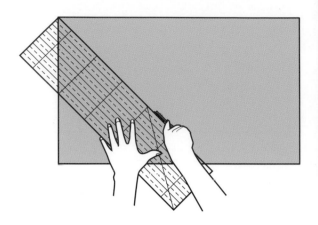

3. Move ruler over 1⅜" from the diagonal cut. Cut again. You should get a bias strip at least 18" in length.

4. Cut one 1⅜" x 18" bias strip per Basket for your size quilt. *Left over fabric can be used for other pieces in block.*

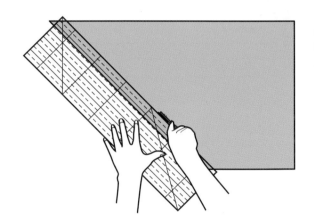

Pieced Squares: Cut 9" strips into 9" x 12" pieces. One piece is enough for four Baskets plus 4 extra ◩.

	Solid Square Setting			Lattice and Cornerstone Setting		
	9" Strips	into	9" x 12" Pieces	9" Strips	into	9" x 12" Pieces
Baby			1	1		2
Lap	1		2	1		2
Twin	2		4	1		3
Double	2		5	2		5
Queen	2		5	2		5
King	2		6	2		6

Top Edge Triangles: Cut 4½" strips into 4½" squares. You need one square for every Basket. If your Basket fabric is a directional fabric, as a basket weave, cut (2) 3" squares for each Basket in place of the 4½" square.

4½"

or

(2) 3" for directional fabric

	Solid Square Setting			Lattice and Cornerstone Setting		
	4½" Strips	into	4½" Squares	4½" Strips	into	4½" Squares
Baby	1		4	1		5
Lap	1		6	1		8
Twin	2		15	2		11
Double	3		20	2		18
Queen	3		20	2		18
King	3		25	3		25

Feet: Cut 3" dark squares from 3" strips or left-over side pieces. You need one piece for every Basket.

	Solid Square Setting			Lattice and Cornerstone Setting		
	3" Strips	into	3" Squares	3" Strips	into	3" Squares
Baby			4			5
Lap	1		6	1		8
Twin	2		15	1		11
Double	2		20	2		18
Queen	2		20	2		18
King	2		25	2		25

Cutting and Sewing Green Fabric for Pieced Leaves

1. Cut one 2" selvage to selvage strip from medium green and dark green. You need a total of 40" from each one.

2. Sew together with ¼" seam.

3. Press seam open.

4. Store in marked plastic bag. Cut off pieces from this strip set when leaf directions call for Pieced Leaf.

5. When pairing pieced strip with interfacing, line up dashed line on interfacing with seam.

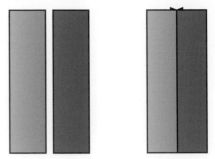

Some parts of flowers are also pieced in this manner.

Cutting Green Fabric for Bias Stems

1. Cut one 9" selvage to selvage strip from medium green and dark green. If you use a green ombre that graduates from medium to dark, cut only that piece.

2. Line up 45º line on 6" x 24" ruler with left selvage edge.

3. Cut on diagonal. Fabric to left of cut can be used for Leaves.

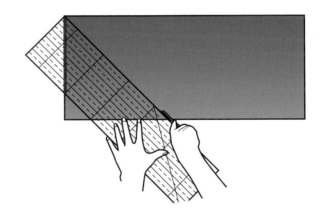

4. Move ruler over 1¼" from diagonal cut. Cut again.

5. Cut eight 1¼" bias strips from each.

6. Store in marked plastic bags, and use when directions call for bias Stem strips.

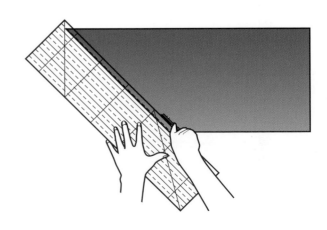

Making Fussy Cuts

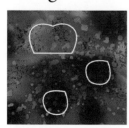

If you have fabric printed with leaves approximately the same size and shape as provided Leaf pattern, use this method. You can also use this method for the centers of flat Roses.

1. Fussy cut leaves or flowers approximately ½" away from outside edges.

2. Trace slightly beyond the outline of leaf or flower on wrong side of fabric with a fine point permanent marking pen.

3. Place dotted fusible side of interfacing on right side of fabric.

4. From wrong side of fabric, sew on inside edge of line with 20 stitches per inch.

5. Trim ⅛" away from stitching lines. Turn right side out, and press with wooden iron.

6. If the image is not visible from the wrong side of the fabric, trace on interfacing through window or light table.

Using Mottled Fabrics

Mottled fabrics are fabrics that have areas of light and dark values. To add interest to your flowers, cut pieces of different values from the same fabric.

Another way to add interest to flowers is to add shading to the petals. Place the darker part of the fabric along the outside edge of the petals.

Handle Pattern
Trace pattern onto template plastic and cut out shape,
or

trace on paper and glue pattern on cardboard.

¼" Seam Allowance

Use a consistent ¼" seam allowance throughout the construction of the quilt. If necessary, adjust the needle position, change the presser foot, or feed the fabric under the presser foot to achieve the ¼". **Complete the ¼" seam allowance test before starting.**

1. Cut (3) 1½" x 6" pieces, and sew the three strips together lengthwise with what you **think** is a ¼" seam.

2. Press the seams in one direction. Make sure no folds occur at the seam when pressing.

3. Place the sewn sample under a ruler and measure its width. **It should measure exactly 3½".** If sample measures smaller than 3½", seam is too large. If sample measures larger than 3½", seam is too small. Adjust the seam allowance and repeat if necessary.

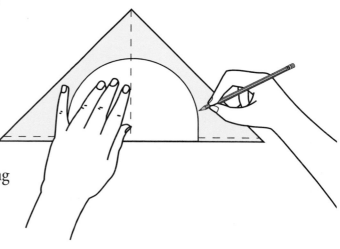

Making the Basket Block

1. Make Handle pattern, including center line. Cut out pattern.

2. With a pencil, draw one diagonal line on 13¼" Background square.

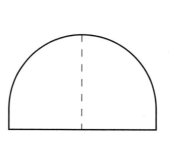
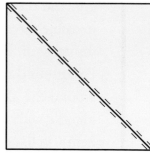

3. Staystitch with seam slightly less than ¼" and 15 stitches per inch on both sides of diagonal line. Press.

4. Cut in half.

5. Fold triangle in half wrong sides together and crease.

6. Place handle pattern on triangle, lining up bottom edges and centers. Trace around curve with a pencil.

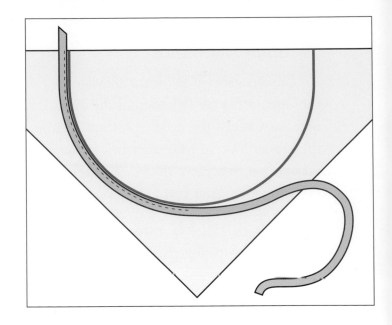

7. Carefully press 1⅜" x 18" dark Basket bias strip wrong sides together.

8. Place raw edges of the folded bias strip on the outside edge of the line. Place folded edge toward outside. Allow 1" extra at end.

9. Use "needle down" on your machine. Working in short sections ahead of the needle, **gently pull** the bias strip to the curve and then sew ¼" seam. **Do not use a scant ¼" seam.**

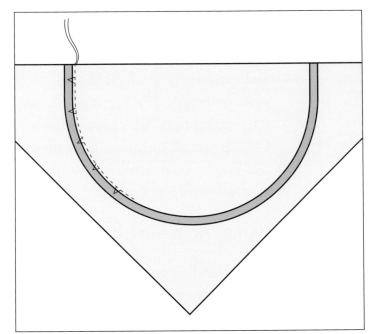

10. Fold strip back over raw edge. Gently **steam press** Handle flat. Trim raw edges ⅛" from seam if they show.

11. Stitch in place by machine or hand. To stitch by machine, select the blind hem stitch. Set the stitch length to 1.0, and the stitch width to 2.0. Place invisible thread on top, and loosen the top tension. Place thread matching the Background in the bobbin. Stitch around the loose edge, catching the Handle with the "bite" of the blind hem stitch.

Sewing Baskets

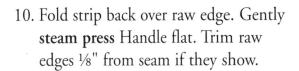

Use a ¼" foot for your Baskets, and thread slightly darker than your fabric so you can see that you are sewing a straight and accurate ¼" seam. Use a fine sharp, #80/12 needle and small stitches, approximately 15 per inch or setting 2.0 on your computerized machine. Do not backstitch, except where indicated.

Follow **Pieced Squares for One Basket** if you want to make each Basket in a different fabric, or make one Basket at a time and finish the appliqued flowers before making the next Basket. If you plan to assembly-line sew, follow **Pieced Squares for Multiple Baskets**, next page. (Complete the ¼" Seam test before starting.)

Pieced Squares for One Basket

1. Place 3" x 9" medium and dark Basket fabrics right sides together.

2. Draw 3" grid. Draw diagonal lines.

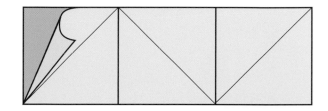

3. Begin sewing ¼" from line. Continue to sew ¼" from diagonal line. Pivot with needle in fabric.

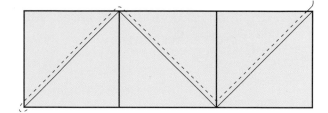

4. Turn and sew ¼" from diagonal line on second side.

5. Press and set seams.

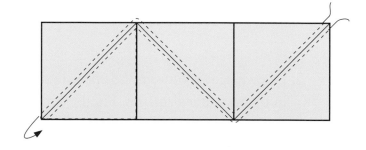

6. Cut apart on straight and diagonal lines.

7. **Turn to Squaring Up instructions, page 34.**

Pieced Squares for Multiple Baskets

1. Place 9" x 12" pieces of medium and dark Basket fabrics right sides together. Place the lightest fabric on top, wrong side up. Press.

2. Place on gridded cutting mat.

3. With 6" x 24" ruler, draw a 3" grid.

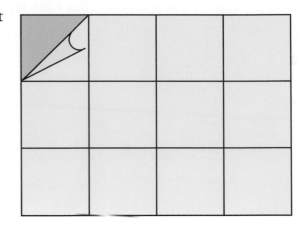

Mark (1) 9" x 12" piece for every 4 Baskets. You will have four extra

4. Beginning in bottom right corner, draw diagonal lines **every other square.**

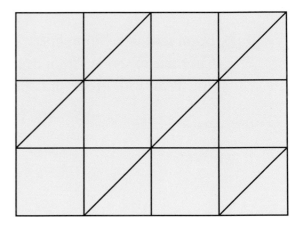

5. Draw diagonal lines in the opposite direction in the unmarked squares. Pin the two pieces together.

6. Place a ¼" foot on your sewing machine, or move the needle for a ¼" seam allowance. Set your machine to fifteen stitches per inch.

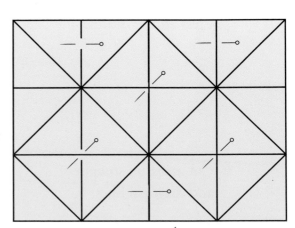

7. Line up ¼" foot on left edge of diagonal line. Stitch. Check that your stitches are ¼" from line.

Start

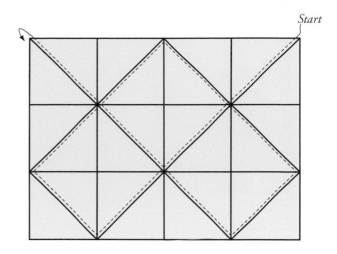

8. Continuously sew ¼" from the diagonal line. Pivot and turn with the needle in the fabric, until you come to the opposite corner.

9. Turn the fabric, line up the ¼" foot on the second side of the line, and continuously sew until you come back to the starting point. Do not backstitch.

10. Press to set the seams.

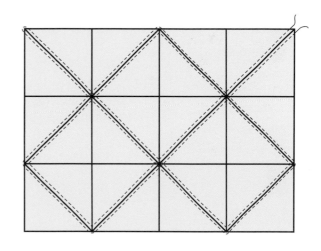

11. Cut apart on 3" square lines. Cut apart on diagonal lines.

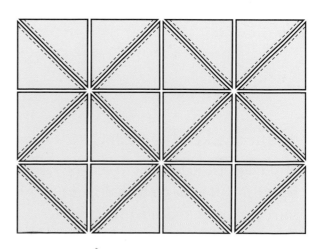

Squaring Pieced Squares to 2½"

Pressing Seams to Dark Side

1. Drop on pressing mat with dark on top.

2. Press to set seam.

3. Open and press seam a second time, toward dark.

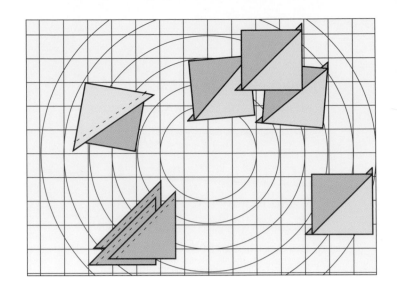

4. Place the 6" Square Up ruler on the Pieced Square so 2½" is centered on the patch. Trim on two sides.

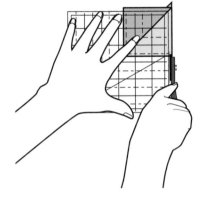

5. Turn and place 2½" on cut edges. Cut remaining two sides, squaring the patch.

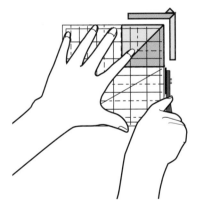

Sewing the Basket Together

1. **Top Edge Triangles:** Cut 4½" dark Basket square into fourths on both diagonals. Leave square together until after second cut.
   Directional fabric: Cut (2) 3" squares directional fabric only once.

4½" Square

Or

(2) 3" Squares

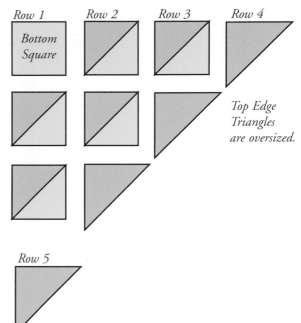

Row 1 · Row 2 · Row 3 · Row 4

Bottom Square

Top Edge Triangles are oversized.

Row 5

2. Lay out pieces for Basket. *If you are making multiple blocks, place four pieces in each stack.*

3. Separate out Row 1 and Row 2. Flip Row 2 onto Row 1. Match square edges. Tip on triangle is oversized, and extends past Pieced Square approximately ⅝".

4. Assembly-line sew with an accurate ¼" seam. Butt pieces close together. Use a stiletto to feed pieces under presser foot.
   If you are making multiple blocks, assembly-line sew rows. Clip the connecting threads after each triangle and stack.

Do not use a scant ¼" seam.

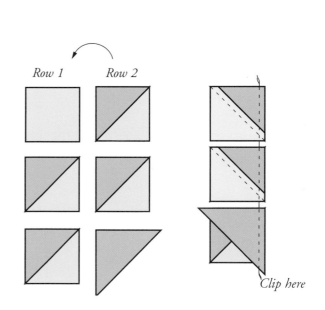

Row 1 · Row 2

Clip here

5. Open Row 1 and Row 2. *Place Row 3, a Pieced Square and Top Edge Triangle, on inside arm of sewing machine for ease in sewing.* Flip Row 3 onto Row 2.

6. Assembly-line sew. *If you are making multiple blocks, clip the connecting threads after each triangle and stack.*

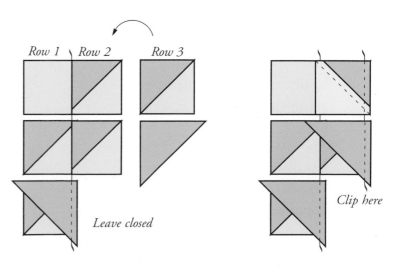

Row 1 · Row 2 · Row 3

Leave closed

Clip here

35

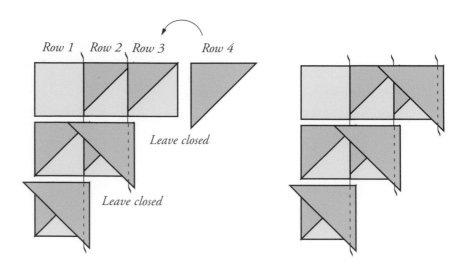

7. Flip Row 4, Top Edge Triangle, onto third row. Carefully line up square edges. Sew.

Leave closed

Leave closed

Pressing the Basket

1. Turn Basket over so it is **wrong side up.** Finger press seams by rows in opposite directions as indicated by arrows.

2. Turn to right side and check for folds in seams. Finger press again.

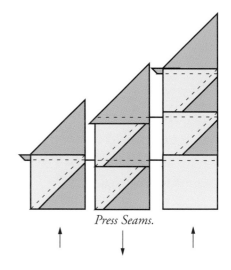

Press Seams.

Sewing Horizontal Rows

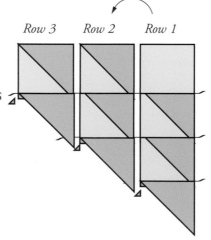

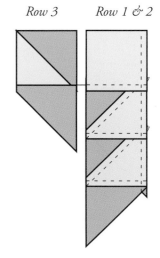

1. Position Basket right side up with Row 1 to right. Trim tips straight with Pieced Square. **Keep your trimming scissors handy and trim any tips that get in the way of your ¼" foot.**

2. Flip Row One right sides together to Row Two. Match and lock seams in opposite directions, and sew together. *Clip connecting threads for multiple Baskets.*

3. Flip Row 2 to Row 3, match and lock seams. Sew Rows Two and Three together. Clip connecting threads.

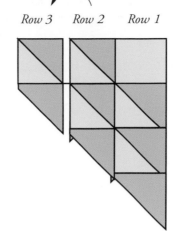

Row 3   *Row 2*   *Row 1*

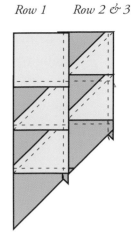

Row 1   *Row 2 & 3*

4. Flip Basket onto Row 5, last Top Edge Triangle, right sides together. Carefully match square edges.

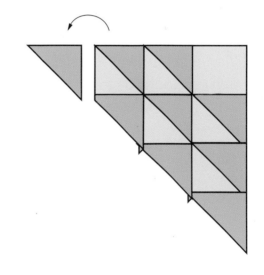

5. Sew.

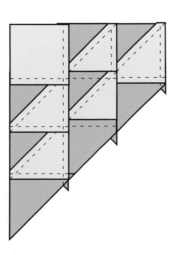

Checking Your Basket

1. Place Basket straight on pressing mat, right side up, lining up Basket with lines on grid. Press seams to one side away from Row 1. "Block" by pressing and stretching so Basket makes perfect 90° angle.

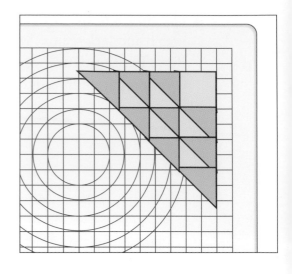

2. Place Basket in corner of gridded cutting mat. Check that Top Edge Triangles were added correctly and block makes a 90° angle. The top edges of the Basket should line up near the 9" lines. If your block meets this criteria, continue on to next page. If your Basket is different, you need to make an adjustment in your seam allowance or pressing technique.

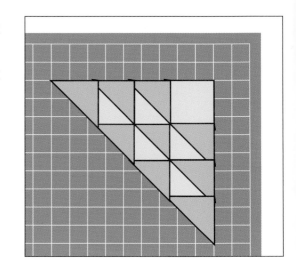

3. **If absolutely necessary, sliver trim outside edges to straighten,** by placing 12½" Square Up ruler on Basket. Center ruler's diagonal line on Basket.

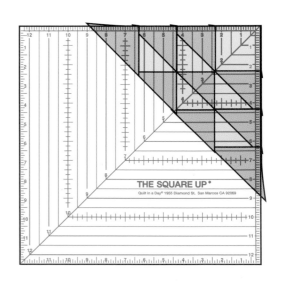

Adding the Feet

1. You need one 3" square per Basket. Carefully cut 3" Dark Basket squares in half on one diagonal. Set half aside.

3" Square

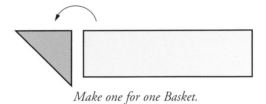

Make one for one Basket.

2. Count out 2¾" x 10" Sides from Background fabric equal to number of Baskets.

3. Flip Sides to Feet, matching straight edges, and sew. *If you are making more than one, assembly-line sew.*

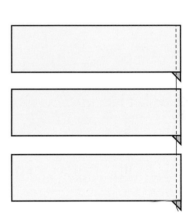

4. With Feet wrong side up, set seams and press toward Feet. Clip apart.

5. Place Basket with Feet. Flip right sides together.

6. Match and lock seams on Bottom Square and Feet. Sew from Feet to top of Basket. Set seams, and press Side away from Basket.

7. From right side, trim tip even with Bottom Square.

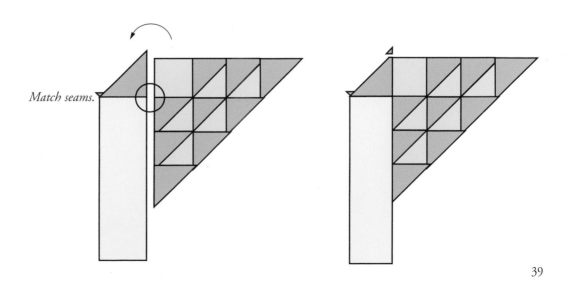

Match seams.

8. Place second half of Feet with Sides and sew.

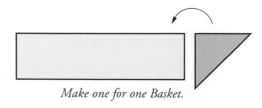

Make one for one Basket.

Assembly-line sew for Multiple Baskets. Press seams toward Feet.

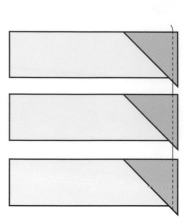

9. Place Feet with Basket, and flip right sides together.

10. Match and lock seams on Bottom Square and Feet. *Assembly-line sew with Side wrong side up, from Feet to top of Basket.*

11. Set seams, and press Side away from Basket.

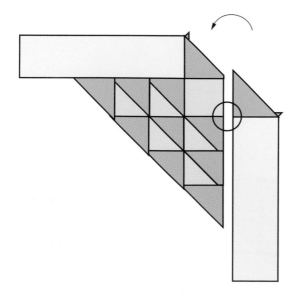

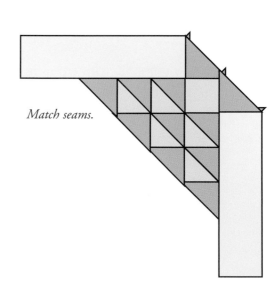

Match seams.

Adding the Bottom

1. Cut 5½" Background squares in half on one diagonal. Use one half per Basket block.

2. Line up 45° line on 6" x 24" ruler with Side on Basket. Lines on ruler should be parallel with seams in Basket. Line up ruler's ¼" line with Feet seam. Cut straight.

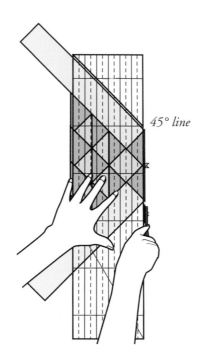

45° line

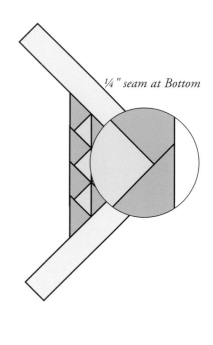

¼ " seam at Bottom

3. Flip Basket right sides together to Bottom. Center Basket on Bottom triangle. Equal tips on both sides should be exposed.

4. Assembly-line sew. Set seam and press toward Bottom.

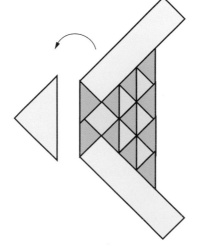

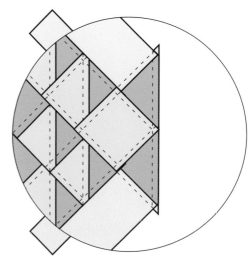

Straightening the Top Edge

1. Put the Basket square on the cutting mat.

2. Line up 6" x 24" ruler with these points:
   - 45° line on Side
   - ¼" line with Top Edge seams
   - Parallel lines on ruler with seams on Basket

3. Cut straight. The bottom edge is squared up after the handle is added.

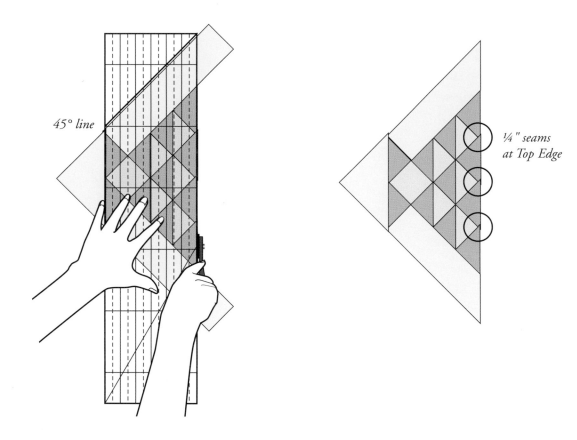

45° line

¼" seams at Top Edge

Sewing the Handle to the Basket

The Handle is sewn to the Basket **after the stem and leaves are added.** Refer to your pattern.

1. Match and pin center on Handle with center seam on Basket.

2. Check that the Handles are equally spaced from the ends of the Basket. Pin.

3. Sew with a ¼" seam.

4. Press seam toward Basket.

Squaring Up Blocks to Consistent Size

1. Place block right side up on cutting mat with Bottom at top.

2. Line up 12½" Square Up ruler's diagonal line with center of Basket, and ruler's outer most points with center seam between Handle and Basket.

3. Place ruler's ¼" lines on Feet seams. Check for at least ¼" seams. Trim on those two sides.
   It's important to square blocks to one consistent size without trimming off the ¼" seam allowance at the Feet. The ideal size is 12½".
   For blocks smaller than 12½", square all blocks to 12⅜" or 12¼".
   For blocks larger than 12½", square all blocks to 12⅝" or 12¾" with a 16" Square Up ruler.

4. Carefully turn mat without disturbing block or ruler. If you can't turn the mat, turn the ruler and block.

5. Trim on remaining two sides to 12½", or your consistent size.

If an occasional block's edge is shy of the measurement, mark it with a pin, and make an adjustment in that seam allowance when sewing the top together.

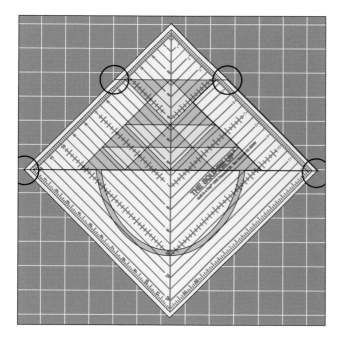
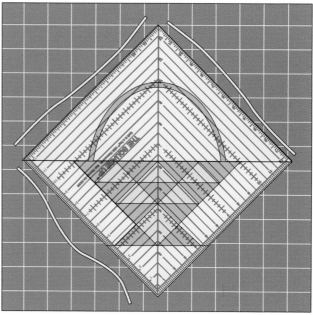

General Instructions for Making Flowers

Gather these supplies and tools for
appliqueing your flowers.

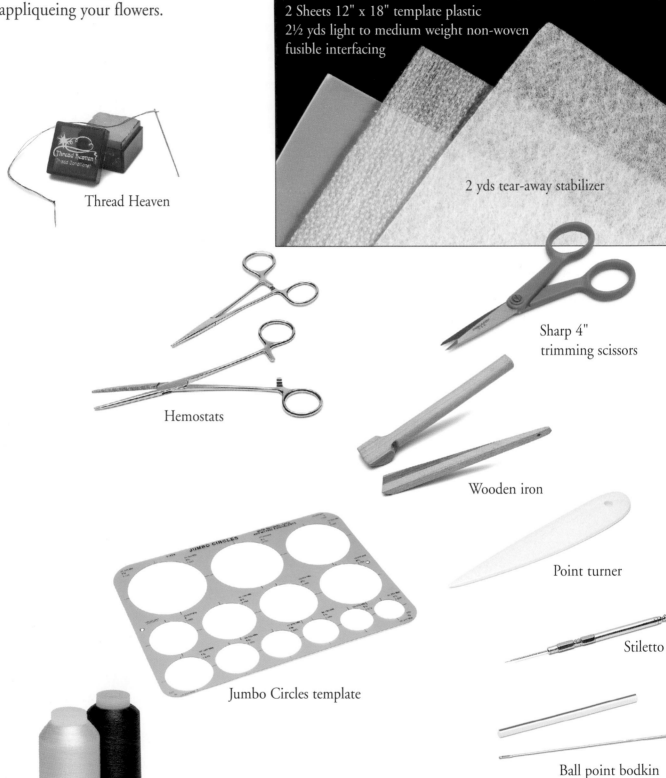

2 Sheets 12" x 18" template plastic
2½ yds light to medium weight non-woven
fusible interfacing

2 yds tear-away stabilizer

Thread Heaven

Hemostats

Sharp 4"
trimming scissors

Wooden iron

Point turner

Stiletto

Jumbo Circles template

Ball point bodkin
and fat straw

Invisible Thread

Permanent marking pen

Sewing Stems from Bias Strips

1. Place Handle piece on Placement sheet. Trace Stem lines with pencil, extending lines under Flower placement. *If you want to use a light table, photocopy first.*

2. Following each Flower's Placement sheet, cut 1¼" bias strips to size. Refer to page 26.

3. Press in half wrong sides together.

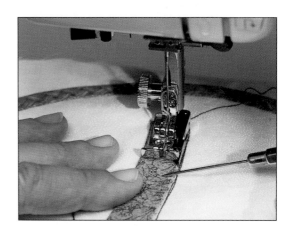

4. If you plan to machine applique your flowers, pin 6" x 9" piece of tear-away stabilizer under Handle piece.

5. Place raw edges of folded bias strip on **inside curve of line.** Sew ¼" seam. Use a stiletto to hold stem in place.

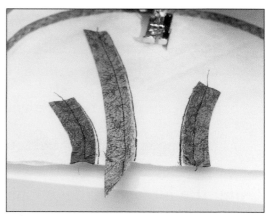

These stems are sewn on the inside curve of line.

6. Fold bias strip back over raw edge and press flat.

7. Sew folded edge to Handle piece with blind hem stitch and invisible thread, or with hand applique. See pages 51–52.

Tracing Patterns

Fusible Interfacing: Use light to medium weight non-woven fusible interfacing and an ultra fine point permanent marker such as a 05 Pigma pen or a fine point Sharpie®. Fusible patterns are indicated by light brown dotted texture on pattern sheets.

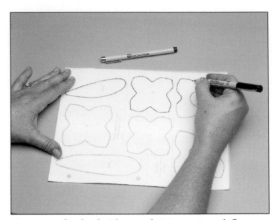

1. Feel interfacing. Find smooth side and "dotted" side. Patterns are traced on smooth side. The textured "dotted" side is the fusible side.

2. Check the permanence of your pen by drawing on smooth side of scrap interfacing and steam pressing dotted side of interfacing to scrap fabric. Substitute pen if it "runs" when pressed.

3. Place a piece of fusible interfacing on the pattern sheet with smooth side up.

4. Trace appropriate pieces with a fine, permanent pen. Include dots and dashed lines.

5. Cut pieces apart as directed by long dashed lines.

Patterns for both Flat and Dimensional flowers are included on the same page. Pieces which are Flat Only or Dimensional Only are separated by a heavy dashed line. Pieces which are shared are separated by a thinner dashed line.

Templates: Use translucent template plastic and a template plastic pencil or a ball point pen for marking. Templates are indicated by light blue shading on pattern pieces.

6. Place template plastic on pattern sheet.

7. Trace appropriate pieces and cut out.

Using the Flower Yardage Chart

1. Pair each interfacing piece on corresponding fabric piece with dotted fusible side against the right side of fabric. The smooth side of interfacing is on top.

2. Cut fabric the same size as the interfacing.

3. Pin in the center of each pattern piece. **Do not press.**

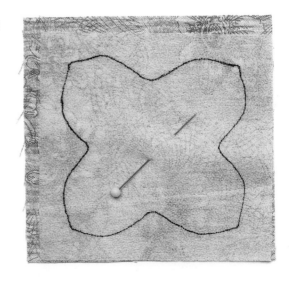

Setting Up your Sewing Machine

1. Select a straight stitch and center needle position on your sewing machine.

2. Use an **"open" metal foot** or teflon foot for visibility. A clear plastic foot tends to pucker the fusible interfacing at this step.

3. Thread with neutral thread on top and in the bobbin. If you do not have balanced tension, use thread to match the fabric.

4. Set your machine with a tight stitch, 20 stitches per inch or 1.8 to 1.5 on computerized sewing machines.

5. If available, use the "needle down" feature. The needle stops in the fabric each time you stop sewing. This feature makes it easy to control sewing on curves and pivoting.

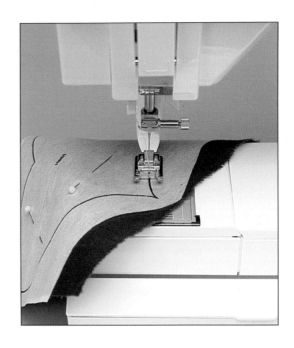

Sewing Around Each Pattern Piece

1. Begin sewing in the middle of a side. Sew on the inside edge of the lines to avoid dark marker lines around the turned pieces. *If the interfacing puckers, lighten the pressure on the presser foot.*

2. Sew slowly on curved pieces, lifting the presser foot and turning the pieces as necessary. Pivot with the needle in the fabric.

3. End by overlapping stitches.

4. Some pieces have an open side. Backstitch and leave open where indicated.

Trimming Each Piece

1. Using sharp, pointed 4" trimming scissors, trim each piece to ⅛" from the stitching. Stitching lines are easily seen from the fabric side.

2. Trim corners, and clip inside curves and outside points.

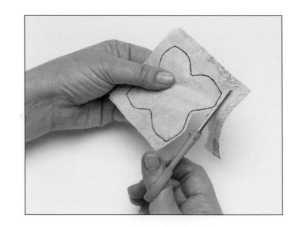

Turning Pieces

Handy tools to use are a ball point bodkin and collection of different sizes of straws or plastic tubing, from ¼" to ½" in diameter. Cut the straw in half. Cut the tube ½" shorter than the bodkin.

1. Turn pieces with an open side through the opening.

2. If the pattern indicated no opening, pull the fusible interfacing away from the fabric.

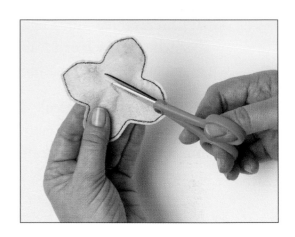

3. Carefully cut a small slit the size of a straw through the fusible interfacing only. Cut slits across the width on the leaves.

4. Insert the straw into the slit. Place straw against fabric.

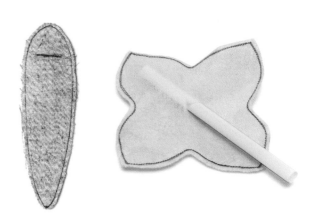

5. Place ball of bodkin on the fabric stretched over the straw end and gently push fabric into straw with the bodkin. This technique begins to turn the piece.

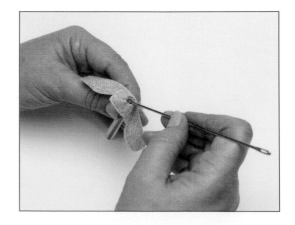

6. Remove the straw and bodkin.

7. If necessary, turn second half with straw and bodkin. Finish turning with fingers.

8. Push out the edges by running a bodkin around the inside. Use a point turner on larger pieces.

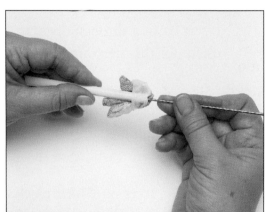

9. Pull out points with stiletto or pin.

Finger Pressing with Wooden Iron

Do not use the iron on this step.

1. Crease fabric edges with a point turner or small wooden "pressing stick," called a wooden iron.

2. From right side, push fabric over interfacing edge.

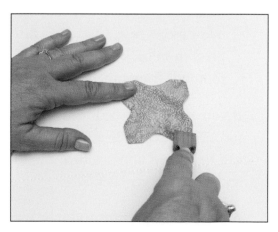

Stuffing With Cotton Batting

Light dimension can be added to largest pieces or specified applique pieces by "stuffing" or padding them with 100% cotton batting. Since pieces are pressed after being "stuffed," cotton batting has to be used as polyester will melt and compress.

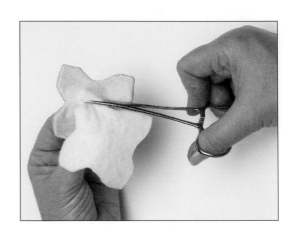

1. Using the **turned piece** as a pattern, cut cotton batting pieces the same shape and size. *Sewing batting in with the applique results in bulky edges.*

2. Insert batting through opening. Hemostats are useful for this step. Smooth edges.

Pressing Pieces in Place

1. Position Handle piece on Placement sheet. Line up fabric with Handle on sheet.

2. Position pieces on Basket block, following outline of Placement sheet underneath. Tuck raw edges under finished pieces.

3. Place block on pressing mat. Carefully slide Placement sheet from under Basket block. Be careful not to touch the ink on the paper with iron.

4. Optional: Place a pressing cloth over block to prevent possible scorching and dirt from iron.

5. Using a cotton setting and steam, firmly press pieces to the background. Misting with water also helps pieces fuse. Once they fuse, turn over and press from back side. "Stuffed pieces" may refuse to bond. If so, pin after attempted pressing.

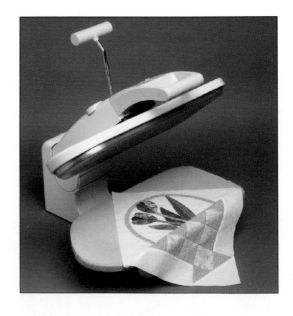

If you are not satisfied with any placement, peel the piece off, reposition, and press again. Edge markings can be coaxed under with a stiletto or pinned under and stitched over later.

An electronic press may also be used.

Outside edges of applique pieces can be finished in a variety of ways. Select your favorite hand or machine method.

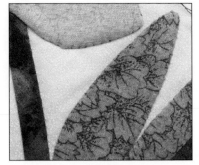
Hand Applique – Front

Hand Applique – Back

Hand Applique

Thread #10 sharp or applique milliner's needle with 18" single strand of regular thread that matches the color of the applique. Pull thread through Thread Heaven or bees wax so it does not tangle. Bring thread up through background fabric and catch just a couple of threads on the fold of the applique. Push needle down through background right above the spot where it came up. Move the needle about ⅛" away, and come up through the background again. Pull stitches firmly but not too tightly. If interfacing shows on the edge of the applique, use tip of needle to tuck it under. Sew a blind stitch that shows just a tiny spot of thread on the front and a slightly longer stitch on the back.

Machine Applique

Use a clear plastic applique foot for visibility. Try out stitches by sewing through several layers of fabric. Stabilize block by placing a 6" x 9" piece of tear-away stabilizer under Handle piece. Tear away the stabilizer once the stitching is completed.

Straight Stitch by Machine

1. Set up your machine top thread with regular, embroidery, topstitching, or hand quilting thread. Select a matching or contrasting color. Use regular thread in the bobbin in the same color as your top thread.

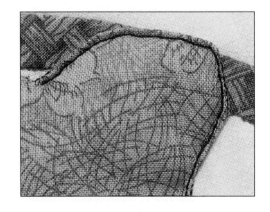

2. Use a #70 needle for regular and embroidery thread, and a #90 needle for topstitching and hand quilting thread.

3. Tighten the top tension for topstitching thread. Adjust the stitch length for each particular piece. Use a small stitch, or setting 2.0, for pieces on curves, as leaves. Use 3.0 for larger pieces, as flowers.

4. Line up the inside edge of the presser foot with the edge of the applique piece. Stitch around each piece 1/16" from the edge. Pull threads with a needle threader, knot, and clip.

Blind Hem or Applique Stitch

1. Set up your machine with nylon invisible thread on the top. Loosen your top tension. Use a small, or #70 needle.

2. Load the bobbin with neutral thread to match the background square.

3. Set your stitch length at 2.0, or 15 stitches per inch, and stitch width at 1.5.

4. Position the needle so the straight stitches line up with the edge on the background fabric, and the "bite" catches the edge of the applique. If the stitch "bites" to the right, begin stitching on the left side of the applique piece. If the stitch "bites" to the left, begin stitching on the right side of the applique piece.

5. At the end of each piece, overlap the stitching, set your stitch width and length to "0", and stitch in place. Clip the threads.

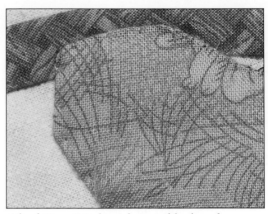

Blind Hem Stitch with invisible thread

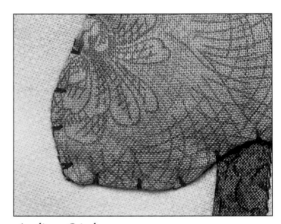

Applique Stitch

Zig-zag Stitch

The zig-zag should catch both the fabric and the background. Use a narrow stitch width and length.

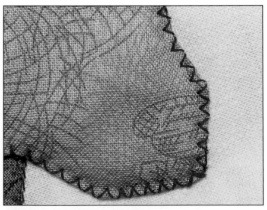

Zig-Zag Stitch

Blanket Stitch

1. Select a coordinating or contrasting color to outline each applique. Use regular or heavy thread in the top and regular matching thread in the bobbin. A suggested stitch length is 3.0 with a stitch width of 3.0.

2. Adjust the stitch so that the straight stitch lines up with the applique on the background fabric, and the "bite" is into the applique. If the blanket stitch "bites" to the right, begin sewing on the left side of the applique. If the blanket stitch "bites" to the left, begin sewing on the right side of the applique. Some computerized sewing machines have the capability to "mirror" the stitch, and "bite" in the opposite direction.

Blanket Stitch

Triple Stitch

The topstitch, or triple stitch, is perfect for veins on flowers. This stitch is often indicated on sewing machines with this symbol:

Triple Stitch

Feather Stitch

The feather stitch adds a decorative touch to leaves and flowers.

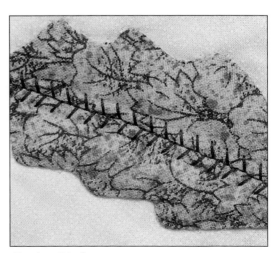

Feather Stitch

Chain Stitching by Machine

Bleeding Heart and Fuchsia call for chain stitching.

1. Spray Handle piece with starch for body. Press.

2. Center Handle on placement sheet. Lines should be visible through the background fabric. Trace lines with pencil.

Chain Stitching

1. Cut a piece of #3 pearl cotton or embroidery floss four times as long as line to be covered, plus a few extra stitches. Fold in half.

2. Match thread to the pearl cotton and set the machine stitch length to 3.0.

3. Place 6" x 9" piece of stabilizer under Handle piece.

4. Place the center of the pearl cotton on one end of the line. Stitch back and forth over the pearl cotton to anchor it.

5. Pull the pearl cotton across the presser foot. Hold the ends of the pearl cotton taut.

6. Take three machine stitches. Stop with the needle in the fabric.

7. Criss-cross the pearl cotton in front of the needle.

8. Stitch over the pearl cotton, and take three machine stitches.

9. Continue to criss-cross and stitch until the line is covered. Backstitch.

10. Perforate the stabilizer by removing the thread from the needle, and sewing on the "chain stitch" with a very small stitch. Pull the paper away.

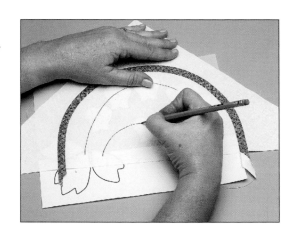

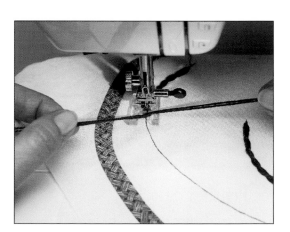

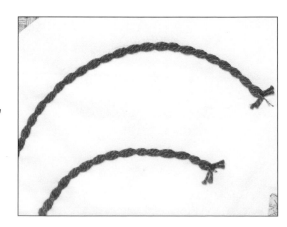

French Knots

1. Use #5 pearl cotton or two to three strands of floss. Bring needle up through fabric at the point where the knot is to be made.

2. Hold the needle close to the fabric and wind the floss two or three times around the point.

3. Hold the floss taut around the needle and insert the needle through the fabric close to the point where the floss came out. Place your thumb over the knot to hold the twist in place and pull the floss through to the underside, bringing the knot snugly against the fabric. Knot on the back side.

Backstitch

1. Use #5 pearl cotton or two strands of embroidery floss. Work from right to left. Bring needle up a short distance from start of line to be covered. Insert it at start of line.

2. Bring needle out an equal distance ahead along line. Draw needle through.

Satin Stitch

1. Bring needle up at one edge of area to be covered, and insert at opposite edge.

2. Return to starting line by carrying floss underneath fabric. Make stitches close enough together to cover background fabric completely.

Outline or Stem Stitch

1. Work from left to right. Bring needle up at end of line to be covered. Insert needle a short distance to the right and bring out a little way to the left at a slight angle.

2. Keep thread above needle.

Making Yo-Yos

1. With your Circle Master, cut a circle twice the desired finished size of your yo-yo plus ½" for seam allowance. For instance, cut a 2½" circle for a 1" yo-yo.

2. Thread a hand sewing needle with a double strand of waxed matching thread, and knot.

3. From the wrong side, turn under the raw edge ¼" and run a long gathering stitch near the folded edge.

4. Turn right side out, gather tightly, flatten, and adjust gathers.

5. Push needle through center, and knot on back. Sew in position on block before cutting thread.

Each flower pattern is six pages long.

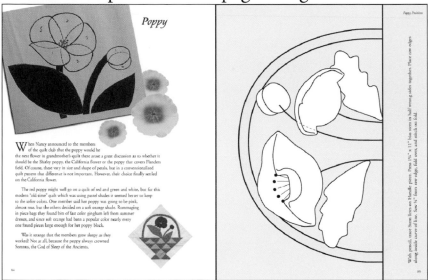

Pages One and Two

The Historical page features a condensed version of the original Nancy Page story and line drawing that appeared in the weekly newspaper. The antique quilt block was made by a reader following Nancy's color suggestions.

The Placement page has stem lines to trace onto your Handle piece, and outlines for positioning completed flowers.

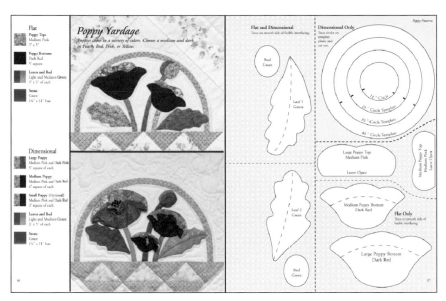

Pages Three and Four

The Flower Yardage page suggests colors and fabrics to use, plus sizes to cut the fabric. Follow Flat or Dimensional instructions, or use a mix of both.

The Pattern sheet has full size patterns to trace in Flat or Dimensional or both. Dotted texture indicates patterns to trace onto fusible interfacing. Patterns on blue are traced onto template plastic and cut out.

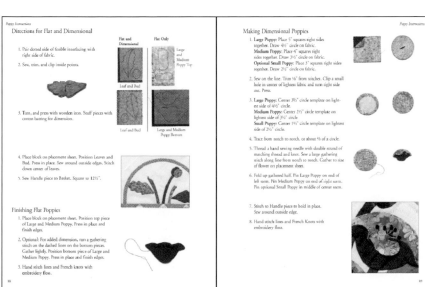

Pages Five and Six

Flower directions begin with instructions for both Flat and Dimensional. Specific instructions for each then follow.

T he first flower used in the Grandmother Quilt was the early spring crocus. At Nancy's suggestion Cynthia used figured yellow. "I wish we could show the deep yellow stigma of the flowers. It is from them we get saffron."

"Oh, have you had saffron cake and buns?" asked Marjorie, who had just returned from a year in England. "We had them over there at Easter time. And I heard that old superstition that saffron dyed linen had health value. Henry VIII had to forbid his people to use the dye. They colored cloth with it, and said it had sanitary value and needed less laundry than white material."

The club laughed over that and while they were still smiling Nancy told them of the first crocus.

"Once upon a time there was a noble youth named Crocus, who loved a shepherdess called Smilax. But, according to the laws of the old Greek gods, Crocus could not stoop to wed a shepherdess. He killed himself in his grief. The Goddess Flora felt so badly for him that she turned both Crocus and Smilax into plants. He became the jaunty yellow flower we know and Smilax was the beautiful vine with tendrils which clings to Crocus. For Greek marriage festivals they used garlands bound together with smilax tendrils."

With pencil, trace Stem lines on Handle piece. Press 1¼" x 8" bias stem in half right sides together.

Flat

Petal A
Dark Purple
3" square

Petal B
Medium Purple
3" square

Petal C
Light Purple
3" square

Leaf D
Dark Green
2" x 4½"

Leaf E
Light Green
2" x 3½"

Pieced Leaf and Stems
Medium and Dark Green
2" x 6" of each
1¼" x 8" bias

Dimensional

Petal A
Dark Purple
3" square

Petal B
Medium Purple
3" square

Petal C
Light Purple
3" square

Leaf D
Dark Green
2" x 4½"

Leaf E
Light Green
2" x 3½"

Pieced Leaf and Stems
Medium and Dark Green
2" x 6" of each
1¼" x 8" bias

Crocus Yardage

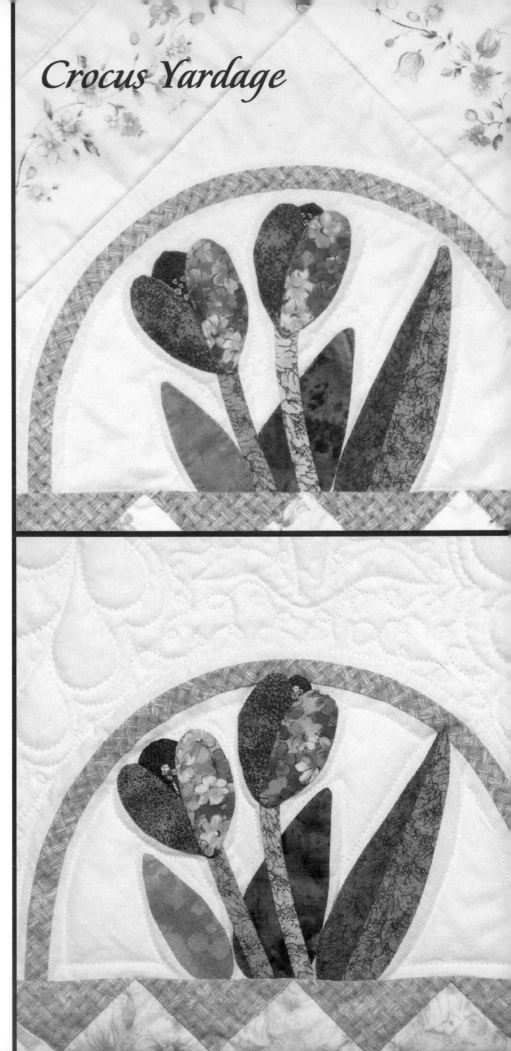

Flat and Dimensional

Trace on smooth side of
fusible interfacing.

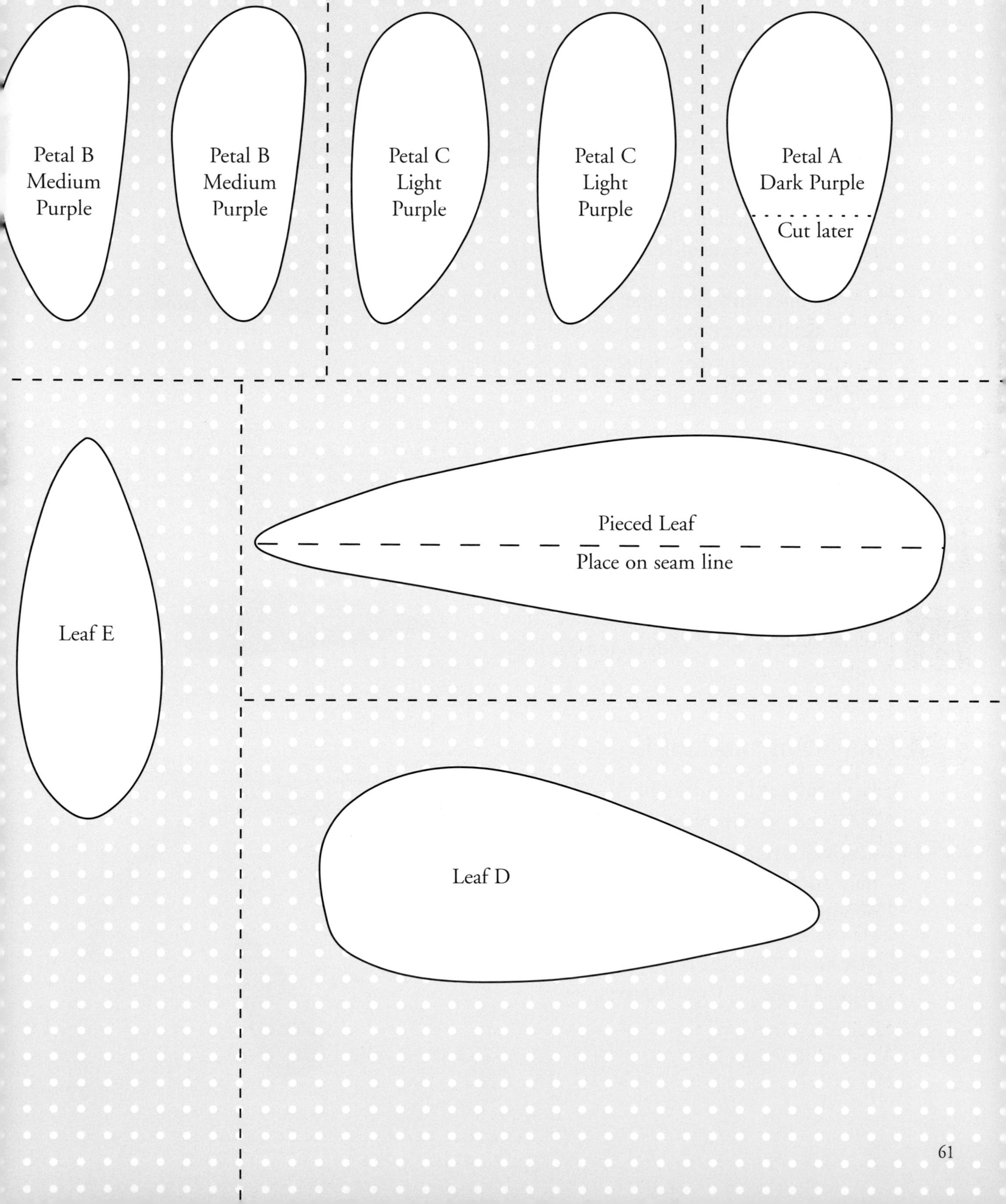

Petal B
Medium
Purple

Petal B
Medium
Purple

Petal C
Light
Purple

Petal C
Light
Purple

Petal A
Dark Purple

Cut later

Leaf E

Pieced Leaf

Place on seam line

Leaf D

Instructions for Flat and Dimensional

1. Place fusible interfacing smooth side up on pattern pieces. *Page 46.*

2. Trace Petals, Leaves, and dashed lines with a permanent marking pen on smooth side of fusible interfacing.

3. Cut pieces apart on dashed lines.

4. Place dotted, fusible side of interfacing on right side of fabrics.

5. Sew on lines with 20 stitches per inch, metal presser foot, and needle down position. Loosen presser foot pressure if interfacing puckers. *Page 47.*

6. Trim ⅛" away from stitched line. Cut a ½" slit in interfacing. Keep hole small as end of straw. *Page 48.*

7. Turn right side out with bodkin and straw. Stuff Petals B and C with cotton batting. *Page 48.*

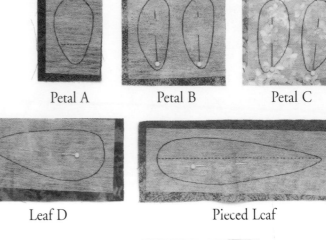

Petal A   Petal B   Petal C

Leaf D   Pieced Leaf

Leaf E

Making Stems and Leaf D

1. Position Leaf D on Handle piece and press in place. Part of Leaf will cover part of Stem line. Turn over, and press on wrong side. *Page 50.*

2. Sew around outside edge. *Pages 51 and 52.* Cut off excess.

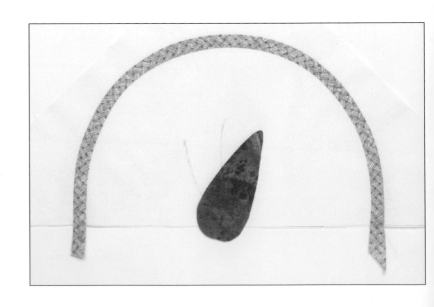

3. **Stem:** Place raw edges along inside curve of line, stitching from bottom edge toward Handle. Fold over, and stitch on fold. *Page 45.*

4. Position Pieced Leaf, press, and sew. Along bottom edge, trim Leaves and Stems from wrong side.

5. Sew Handle piece to Basket. Square block to 12½". *Page 42.*

Making the Crocus

1. Cut Petal A on the line.

Left Crocus

Right Crocus

2. Using the placement sheet as a guide, arrange and press Petals A on Handle piece.

3. Arrange two Petals B, overlapping Petals A. Position with rounded ends at top.

4. Press in place with steam. Turn over and press from back.

5. Position Petals C on Petals A and B. Press again.

6. Sew around outside edges.

7. Sew French Knots in center of open Crocus with gold embroidery floss or #5 pearl cotton. *Page 55.*

Fuchsia

There was a most beautiful display of colors when the Nancy Page club assembled for their weekly meeting. The crocus block made last week was duly admired. The first part of Grandmother's Garden quilt was finished. Cynthia viewed her work with pride.

As they sewed busily, Nancy told them the story of the fuchsia. As Christ walked to the hill where He was crucified, drops of blood fell from His thorn-crowned brow. As they fell, a beautiful flower with crimson heart and wrapping of purple robe of royalty sprang up. Because they grew in the shadow of the cross they tremble and quiver in any breeze as if they were in agony.

When the story was finished they were silent for a moment. Then, "What flower do we make next week Nancy?" "Perhaps you can guess when I tell you that I want you to come prepared to answer roll call with a quotation about a rose."

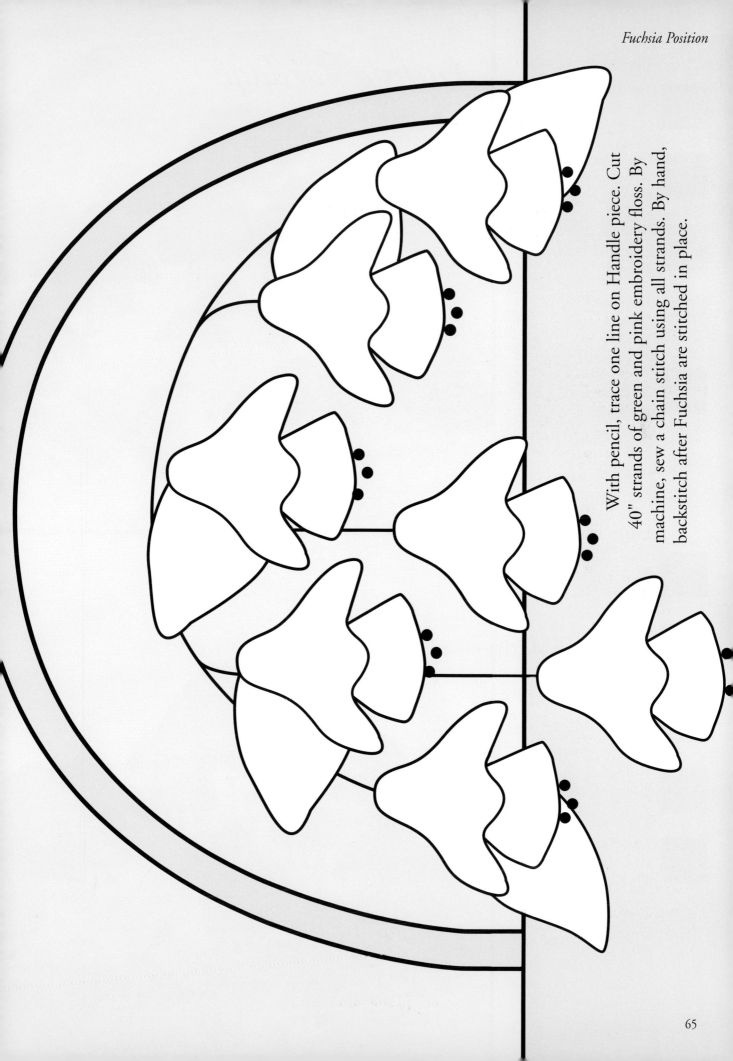

Fuchsia Position

With pencil, trace one line on Handle piece. Cut 40" strands of green and pink embroidery floss. By machine, sew a chain stitch using all strands. By hand, backstitch after Fuchsia are stitched in place.

Flat

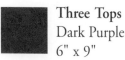

Three Tops
Dark Purple
6" x 9"

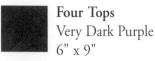

Four Tops
Very Dark Purple
6" x 9"

Bottoms
Fuchsia
3½" x 8"

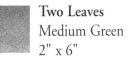

Two Leaves
Medium Green
2" x 6"

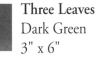

Three Leaves
Dark Green
3" x 6"

Dimensional

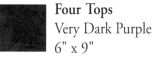

Three Tops
Dark Purple
6" x 9"

Four Tops
Very Dark Purple
6" x 9"

Bottoms
Fuchsia
(7) 2½" x 3½"

Two Leaves
Medium Green
2" x 6"

Three Leaves
Dark Green
3" x 6"

Fuchsia Yardage

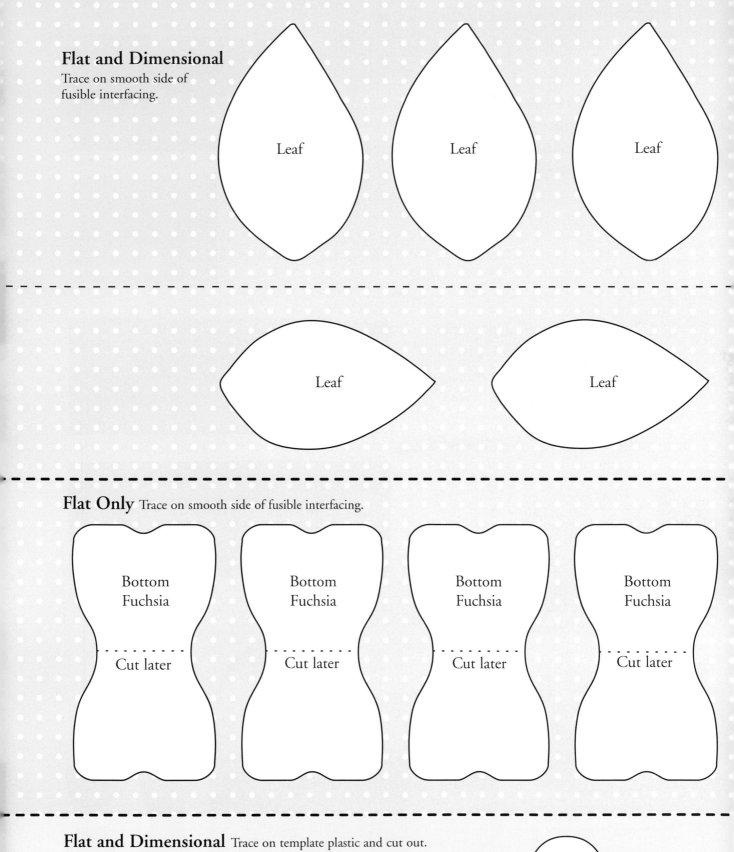

Flat and Dimensional
Trace on smooth side of fusible interfacing.

Leaf

Leaf

Leaf

Leaf

Leaf

Flat Only Trace on smooth side of fusible interfacing.

Bottom Fuchsia

Cut later

Bottom Fuchsia

Cut later

Bottom Fuchsia

Cut later

Bottom Fuchsia

Cut later

Flat and Dimensional Trace on template plastic and cut out.

Top
Flat and Dimensional
Dark Purple

Directions for Flat and Dimensional

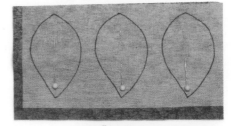

Flat and Dimensional

1. Sew Handle piece to Basket. Square block to 12½".

2. **Leaves:** Place dotted fusible side of traced Leaves on right side of fabric. Sew on lines, trim, turn, and press with wooden iron. Fuse in place, and sew around outside edges.

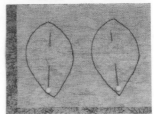

Leaves

3. **Tops:** Fold 6" x 9" dark purple strip in half right sides together. Press. Trace three tops with ½" between each, and pin. Trace four on very dark purple strip. Sew on drawn lines with matching thread.

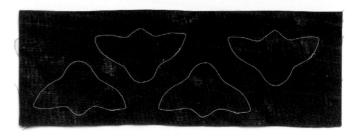

4. Trim seams to ⅛". Cut small opening on one side of fabric. This side is now the back side. Turn right side out and press. Stuff with cotton batting.

Finishing Flat Fuchsia

1. **Bottoms:** Place dotted fusible side of traced Bottoms on right side of fabric. Sew on lines, trim, turn, and press with wooden iron.

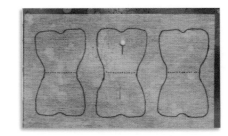

2. Cut each Bottom in half on dotted line and stuff with cotton batting.

3. Position Bottoms and Leaves, and fuse in place. Pin Tops in place, and sew around outside edges.

4. **Stamens:** With floss or pearl cotton, embroider straight lines with French Knots at the ends.

Finishing Dimensional Fuchsia

1. **Bottoms:** Fold 2½" x 3½" Fuchsia pieces in half width-wise. Stitch ¼" seam on 2½" side. Backstitch on each end. Finger press seams open.

2. Turn top half of tube right side out, using your finger or pencil eraser to help form shape.

3. Hand stitch a long gathering stitch around raw edges. Pull tight and knot, forming a small cap shape. With attached thread, sew in place on Handle piece.

4. Using placement sheet, tuck gathered edge of Bottoms under Tops, and pin each in place. Allow space below for embroidered Stamens.

5. Hand stitch Top in place, following arrows.

6. Tack Bottom in place at each dot. Stitch along bottom edge of Top.

7. **Stamens:** With floss or pearl cotton, embroider straight lines with French Knots at the ends.

Rose

T he Nancy Page Quilt club had
just assembled when one of the
members went to the piano and sang, "My Love Is Like a Red, Red Rose." That started the
afternoon and the hours bloomed with tales of roses even as the gardens of Omar blossomed
that he might gather the petals for his precious attar of roses.

One member told of the Persian belief that a nightingale utters a plaintive cry whenever a
rose, the object of its love, is plucked. The English War of Roses, which ended only when
Elizabeth of York was married to Henry the Seventh of the house of Lancaster, thus uniting
the white and the red rose, was recalled. Martin Luther's love for roses which made him choose
a rose as his seal was cited. "Rose leaf skin," "rosy cheeks," "rosebud mouth" showed how like
unto a rose a face is. The club had so much to talk about they could scarcely settle to work.
Nancy had four of them using the same pattern.

"These four rose basket blocks will be the four corners of the pieced part of quilt.
They are put there in memory of my grandmother's garden. She had a rose bush or tree at
each corner of her garden plot. I can still see the four rose sentinels standing guard."

With pencil, trace Stem lines on Handle piece. Press 1¼" x 10" bias stem in half wrong sides together. Place raw edges along inside curve of line. Sew ¼" from raw edge, fold over, and stitch on fold.

Flat

Bud and Base A
Dark Peach
2½" square
4½" square

Petal B
Light Peach
4" square

Petal C
Medium Peach
3" square

Center
Fussy Cut
1" fussy cut

Calyx
Green
2" square

Stems and Leaves
1¼" x 10" bias
3" x 8" or fussy cuts

Dimensional

Bud and Base A
Dark Peach
2½" square
4½" square

Petal B
Light Peach
3" x 9"

Petal C
Medium Peach
2½" x 12"

Center
Dark Peach
2½" x 9"

Calyx
Green
2" x 6"

Stems and Leaves
1¼" x 10" bias
3" x 8" or fussy cuts

Rose Yardage

The Roses are made from three shades of pink, yellow, peach, or red. From each color family, designate a dark, medium, and light.

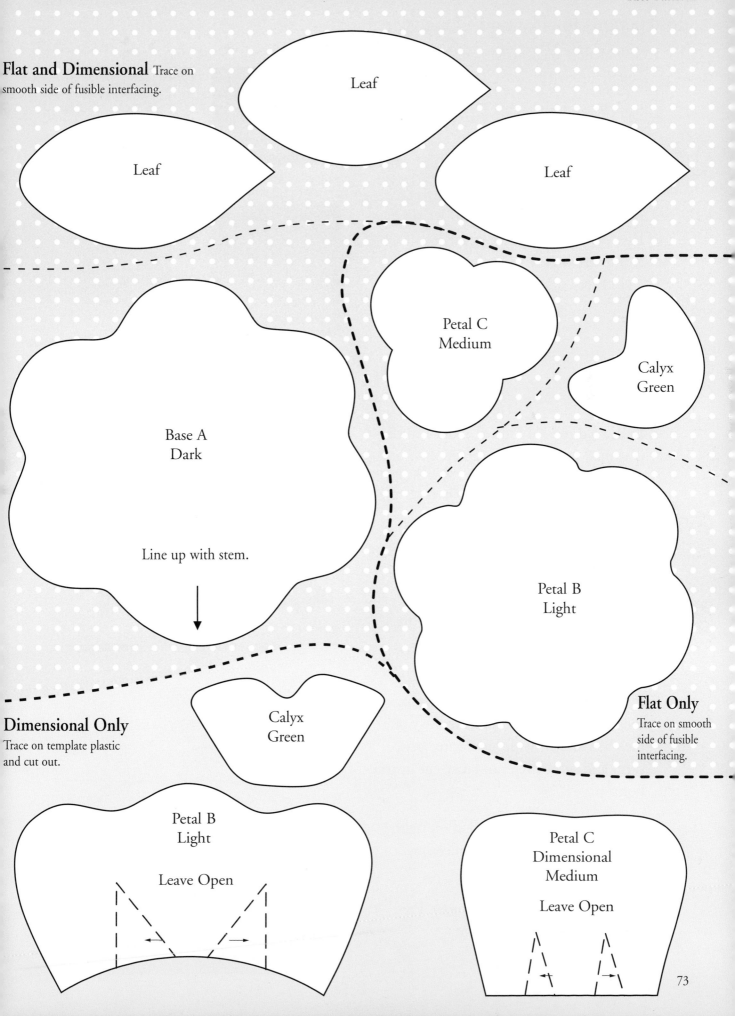

Flat and Dimensional Trace on
smooth side of fusible interfacing.

Leaf

Leaf

Leaf

Petal C
Medium

Calyx
Green

Base A
Dark

Line up with stem.

Petal B
Light

Flat Only

Trace on smooth
side of fusible
interfacing.

Dimensional Only

Trace on template plastic
and cut out.

Calyx
Green

Petal B
Light

Leave Open

Petal C
Dimensional
Medium

Leave Open

Instructions for Flat and Dimensional

1. Sew Handle piece to Basket. Square up to 12½".

2. Pair dotted fusible side of fusible interfacing with right side of fabric.

3. Sew on lines, trim, turn, and press with wooden iron. Stuff Base A, Petal C, and Leaves with cotton batting. Position Base A and Leaves, and press in place.

Flat and Dimensional

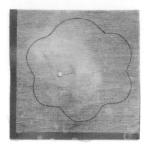

Three Leaves

Flat Only

Petal B

Petal C

Base A

Calyx

4. **Bud:** Fold the 2½" square in half on the diagonal, wrong sides together.

5. Fold the two corners over, following the photos.

6. Thread a hand sewing needle with a double strand of thread. Stitch loosely along bottom edge. Pull loosely for Flat bud, and knot. Pull tight for a Dimensional finish.

Flat   Dimensional

Finishing the Flat Rose

1. **Fussy cut Center:** From a floral print, rough cut one flower approximately one inch across. Pair with interfacing, sew, trim, and turn. (Refer to Fussy cut instructions, page 27.)

2. **Bud and Calyx:** Position Bud on right stem. Place Calyx on top, concealing stitches. Sew in place.

3. Stack Petals in alphabetical order. Press, and sew around outside edges.

Finishing Dimensional Rose

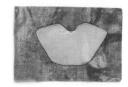

1. **Calyx:** Fold 2" x 6" green strip in half right sides together.

2. Trace one Dimensional Calyx, and sew on lines with matching thread. Trim, turn, and press.

3. Wrap Calyx around Bud, concealing stitches. Pin together. From back side, tack edges together.

4. Position Bud on block, and tack bottom of Calyx, center, and top of Bud.

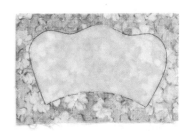

5. **Petal B:** Fold 3" x 9" strip in half right sides together, and trace one Petal B.

6. **Petal C:** Fold 2½" x 12" strip in half right sides together, and trace two Petals C.

7. Sew on traced lines, leaving bottom edges open. Trim, turn, and press. Cut cotton batting ½" shorter than Petals C, and stuff.

8. On Petal B, hand tack two small tucks along bottom raw edge. Use attached thread to sew to top half of Base A.

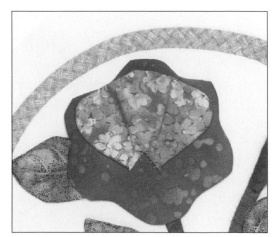

9. On Petals C, tack two small tucks along raw edge, and use attached thread to sew side by side to Base.

10. **Center:** Fold 2½" x 9" strip in half lengthwise right sides together. Placing the folded edge along the top, sew the right side with a ¼" seam. On the left side, begin stitching along the bottom about 1" from left edge, indicated by the arrow. Continue stitching a curved line up to the folded edge.

11. Trim corner. Turn right side out. On right end, measure ½" up and mark dot. Mark second dot on left end ¼" up. Draw line from dot to dot.

12. Starting on right side, roll end tightly 1", and tack on line. Take long running stitches along line. Stop stitching at left dot, and pull gathering thread to half the original length.

Trim

13. Roll bud into spiral shape keeping right rolled end lower. Tack together and knot. Trim excess along raw edge.

14. Roll over top folded edge.

15. Pin in place on top half of Petals. Arrange curved end to conceal raw edges, and sew in place.

16. On Petals C, curl under outside edges and pin in place. Secure with stitches.

Color Selection for Rose Blocks

In the original quilt by Nancy Page, there were four Rose blocks, each in a different color, for each corner. If you plan to make a twenty block quilt, layer cut and make four Roses. If you plan to make a smaller quilt, you may want to make only one Rose. Use leaf patterns provided or make fussy cut leaves. Notice the three different values used in each color family.

Harebell

A s the quilt club members assembled for their weekly meeting they heard strains of "Blue Bells of Scotland." That gave them the flower of the day. It was Jeannie's turn to make the block and she exclaimed in pleasure over the dainty blue bells which Nancy had designed. She said she could almost see them swaying on their slender stems in the breeze among the grasses and flowers.

As they stitched, Nancy told them this flower was called St. George's flower, since it was in blossom on his day, April 23, and since its blue was like the ocean of which he was the patron saint.

Its blue is said to stand for purity. One other delightfully whimsical tale says "it is a fairy flower sending silver music when good fairies ring their chimes for vagrant butterflies."

With pencil, trace Stem lines on Handle piece. Press 1¼" x 8" bias stem in half right sides together. Place raw edges along inside curve of line. Sew ¼" from raw edge, fold over, and stitch on fold.

Flat

Flower and Buds
Dark Blue
3½" square
2" x 3"

Flower
Medium Blue
3½" square

Flower
Medium Lavender
3½" square

Folded Flower
Medium and Dark Lavender
3½" square of each

Stems and Bud
1¼" x 8" bias
1¼" x 3"

Folded Leaves
3" x 5" of each

Dimensional

Flower A and Buds
Dark Blue
3½" x 7"
2" x 3"

Flower A
Medium Blue
3½" x 7"

Flower A
Medium Lavender
3½" x 7"

Folded Flower
Medium and Dark
Lavender
3½" square of each

Stems and Bud
1¼" x 8" bias
1¼" x 3"

Folded Leaves
3" x 5" of each

Harebell Yardage

The color varies from clear medium blue to deep cobalt to pale blue, or violet.

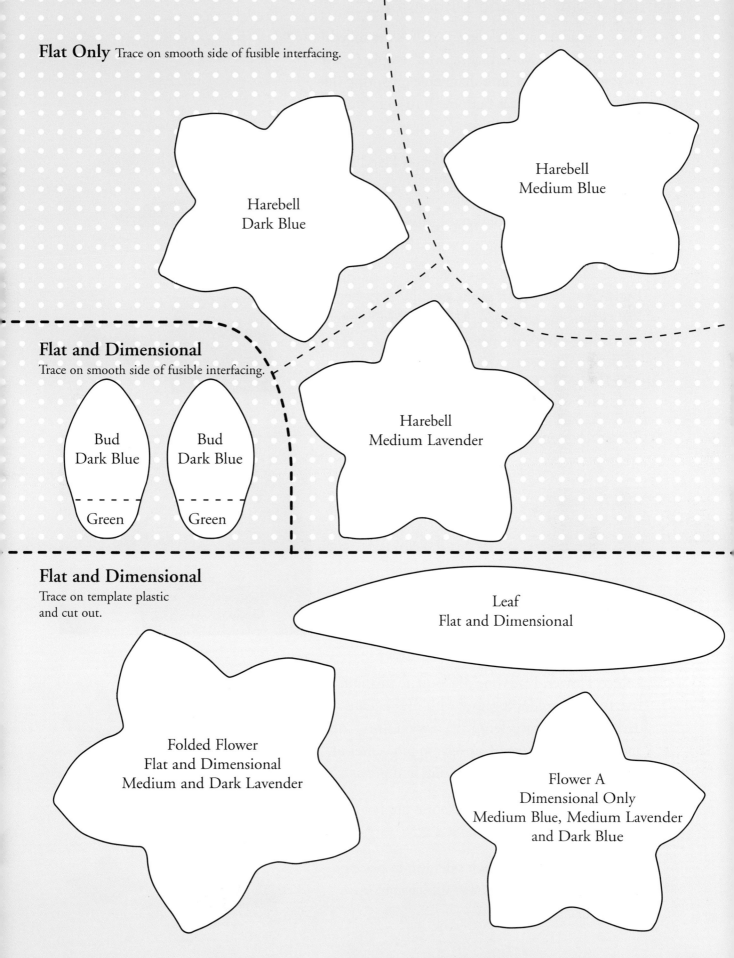

Flat Only Trace on smooth side of fusible interfacing.

Harebell
Dark Blue

Harebell
Medium Blue

Flat and Dimensional

Trace on smooth side of fusible interfacing.

Bud
Dark Blue

Green

Bud
Dark Blue

Green

Harebell
Medium Lavender

Flat and Dimensional

Trace on template plastic
and cut out.

Leaf
Flat and Dimensional

Folded Flower
Flat and Dimensional
Medium and Dark Lavender

Flower A
Dimensional Only
Medium Blue, Medium Lavender
and Dark Blue

Instructions for Flat and Dimensional

1. Place medium and dark greens right sides together. Trace two Leaves on fabric with template. Sew on lines and trim. Cut a small hole on wrong side of medium green near bottom. Turn right side out with bodkin and straw.

2. Fold over tops of Leaves. Position on Handle piece. Sew in place.

3. Sew Handle piece to Basket. Square to 12½".

Flat and Dimensional

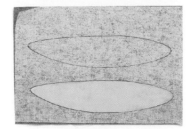

4. **Buds:** Sew 3" strips of green and blue together. Press seams toward green. Match dashed line on interfacing with seam line on Bud.

5. Sew, trim, turn, press with wooden iron, and stuff. Fuse in place, and finish outside edges.

6. Backstitch Stems connecting Buds after Flowers are in place.

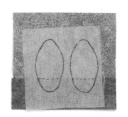

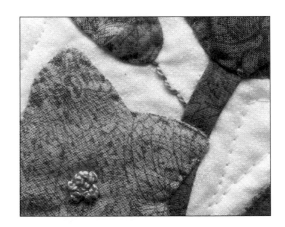

7. **Folded Flower:** Place one 3½" square medium lavender right sides together with 3½" square dark lavender. Trace Template, sew on lines, trim, and clip inside curves. Cut opening in center of lightest fabric, turn right side out, and press.

8. Position Flower with lightest fabric up. Fold bottom half up.

9. Make a small tuck on each side. Pin in place on Stem. Sew outside edges. For dimension, leave front petals unsewn.

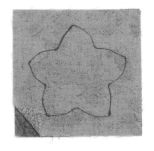

Finishing Flat Harebells

1. Pair dotted side of marked interfacing with right side of 3½" squares. Sew, trim, and clip inside curves. Turn, and press with wooden iron. Stuff with cotton batting.

2. Arrange flowers and fuse in place. Sew around outside edges.

3. Finish centers of flowers with yellow French knots.

Finishing Dimensional Harebells

1. **Template A Flowers:** Fold three 3½" x 7" pieces in half right sides together. Trace three Template A on wrong side of fabric.

2. Stitch on traced lines, trim, and clip inside curves. Turn, and press with wooden iron.

3. Draw 1" circle in center of side with opening. (Use Circle Master or quarter.) Stuff. With double strand of matching thread, sew long stitches along circle, and gather slightly. Knot.

4. Arrange flowers and sew around outside edges.

5. Finish centers of flowers with yellow French knots.

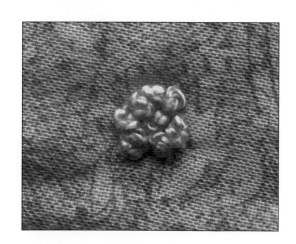

Poppy

When Nancy announced to the members
of the quilt club that the poppy would be
the next flower in Grandmother's Garden quilt there arose a great discussion as to
whether it should be the Shirley poppy, the California flower or the poppy that covers Flanders field. Of course, these vary in size and shape of petals, but in a conven-
tionalized quilt pattern that difference is not important. However, their choice final-
ly settled on the California flower.

The red poppy might well go on a quilt of red and green and white, but for this
modern "old-time" quilt which was using pastel shades it seemed better to keep
to the softer colors. One member said her poppy was going to be pink,
almost rose, but the others decided on a soft orange shade. Rummaging
in piece bags they found bits of fast color gingham left from summer
dresses, and since soft orange had been a popular color nearly every
one found pieces large enough for her poppy block.

Was it strange that the members grew sleepy as they
worked? Not at all, because the poppy always crowned
Somnus, the God of Sleep of the Ancients.

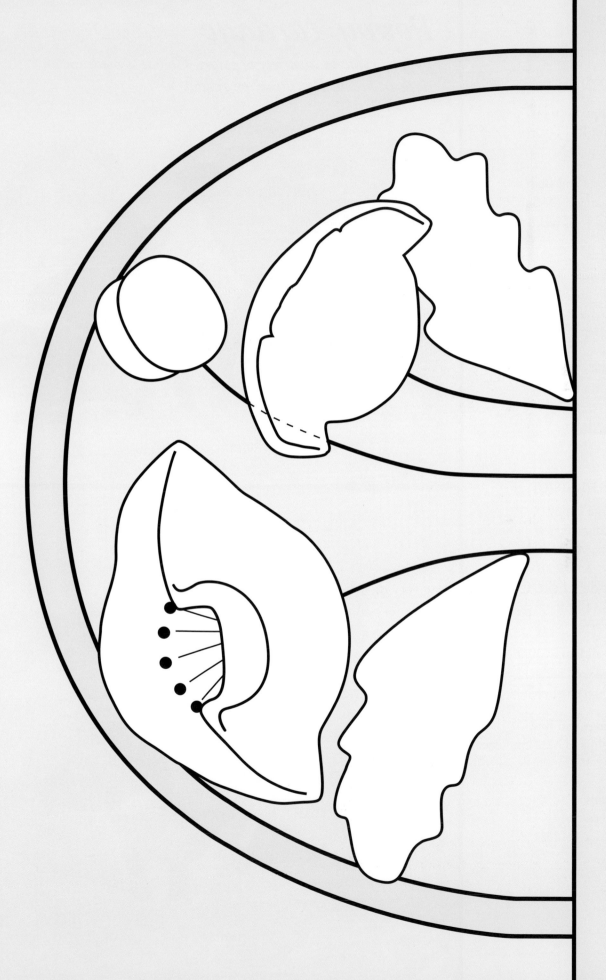

With pencil, trace Stem lines on Handle piece. Press 1¼" x 11" bias stem in half wrong sides together. Place raw edges along inside curve of line. Sew ¼" from raw edge, fold over, and stitch on fold.

Flat

Poppy Tops
Medium Pink
3" x 5"

Poppy Bottoms
Dark Red
5" square

Leaves and Bud
Light and Medium Green
3" x 5" of each

Stems
Green
1¼" x 11" bias

Dimensional

Large Poppy
Medium Pink and Dark Pink
5" square of each

Medium Poppy
Medium Pink and Dark Red
4" square of each

Small Poppy (Optional)
Medium Pink and Dark Red
3" square of each

Leaves and Bud
Light and Medium Green
3" x 5" of each

Stems
Green
1¼" x 11" bias

Poppy Yardage

Poppies come in a variety of colors. Choose a medium and dark in Peach, Red, Pink, or Yellow.

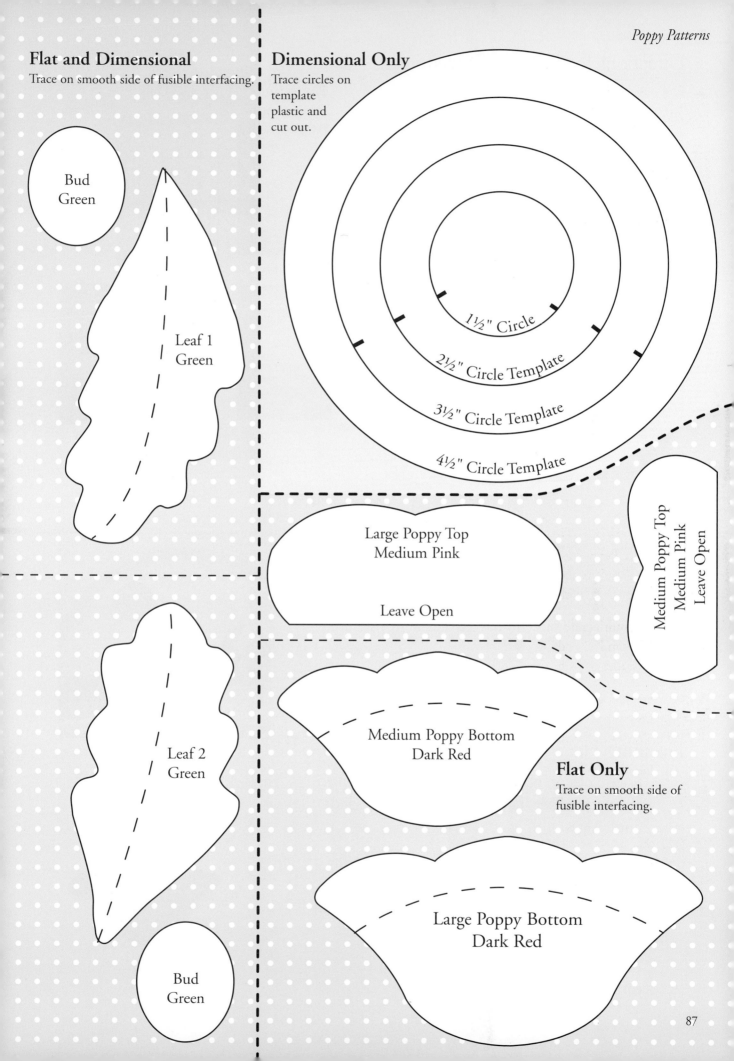

Flat and Dimensional
Trace on smooth side of fusible interfacing.

Bud
Green

Leaf 1
Green

Dimensional Only
Trace circles on template plastic and cut out.

1½" Circle

2½" Circle Template

3½" Circle Template

4½" Circle Template

Large Poppy Top
Medium Pink

Leave Open

Medium Poppy Top
Medium Pink
Leave Open

Leaf 2
Green

Medium Poppy Bottom
Dark Red

Flat Only
Trace on smooth side of fusible interfacing.

Bud
Green

Large Poppy Bottom
Dark Red

Directions for Flat and Dimensional

1. Pair dotted side of fusible interfacing with right side of fabric.

2. Sew, trim, and clip inside points.

3. Turn, and press with wooden iron. Stuff pieces with cotton batting for dimension.

Flat and Dimensional

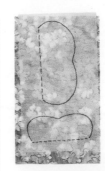

Leaf and Bud

Leaf and Bud

Flat Only

Large and Medium Poppy Top

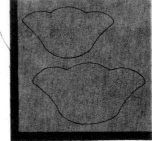

Large and Medium Poppy Bottom

4. Place block on placement sheet. Position Leaves and Bud. Press in place. Sew around outside edges. Stitch down center of leaves.

5. Sew Handle piece to Basket. Square to 12½".

Finishing Flat Poppies

1. Place block on placement sheet. Position top piece of Large and Medium Poppy. Press in place and finish edges.

2. Optional: For added dimension, run a gathering stitch on the dashed lines on the bottom pieces. Gather lightly. Position bottom piece of Large and Medium Poppy. Press in place and finish edges.

3. Hand stitch lines and French knots with embroidery floss.

Making Dimensional Poppies

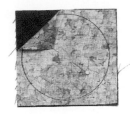

1. **Large Poppy:** Place 5" squares right sides together. Draw 4½" circle on fabric.
   Medium Poppy: Place 4" squares right sides together. Draw 3½" circle on fabric.
   Optional Small Poppy: Place 3" squares right sides together. Draw 2½" circle on fabric.

2. Sew on the line. Trim ⅛" from stitches. Clip a small hole in center of lightest fabric and turn right side out. Press.

3. **Large Poppy:** Center 3½" circle template on lightest side of 4½" circle.
   Medium Poppy: Center 2½" circle template on lightest side of 3½" circle.
   Small Poppy: Center 1½" circle template on lightest side of 2½" circle.

4. Trace from notch to notch, or about ⅔ of a circle.

5. Thread a hand sewing needle with double strand of matching thread and knot. Sew a large gathering stitch along line from notch to notch. Gather to size of flower on placement sheet.

6. Fold up gathered half. Pin Large Poppy on end of left stem. Pin Medium Poppy on end of right stem. Pin optional Small Poppy in middle of center stem.

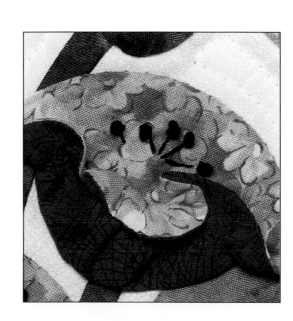

7. Stitch to Handle piece to hold in place. Sew around outside edge.

8. Hand stitch lines and French Knots with embroidery floss.

Pansy

"There is pansies—that's for thought." Every member of the club who was making Grandmother's Garden quilt had begged Nancy to design the pansy block. One member wanted to make it because she had some fast color print in lavender. Another had some yellow and black print she wanted to use. Dorothea chose bits of left-over purple from the fuchsia block and scraps of figured yellow from the crocus. And one artistic soul made a success of a combination of figured soft blue and lavenders. In fact, the choice seemed to be limited only by the dominant note of color in the room in which the finished quilt would be put or by the scraps on hand.

Oberon, you may remember, told Puck to place a pansy on the sleeping eyes of Titania in order that she might fall in love with the first object she saw when she awoke. Nancy's club all fell in love with their pansy blocks.

Pansy Position

With pencil, trace Stem line on Handle piece. Press 1¼" x 3" bias stem in half wrong sides together. Place raw edges along inside curve of line. Sew ¼" from raw edge, fold over, and stitch on fold.

91

Flat

Top Petal A

Dark Lavender, Fuchsia
2½" x 4" of each

Center Petal B

Light Yellow, Fuchsia
2½" x 4" of each

Bottom Petal C

Very Dark Purple
Two 2½" x 3"

Stem

Green
1¼" x 3" bias

Fusible Leaf

Green
2½" x 4½"

Folded Leaves

Medium and Dark
4½" x 5½" of each

Dimensional

Top Petal A

Dark Yellow,
Medium Purple, Fuchsia
2½" x 4" of each

Center Petal B

Light Yellow, Light
Purple, Fuchsia
2½" x 8" of each

Bottom Petal C

Very Dark Purple
Three 2½" x 3"

Stem

1¼" x 3" bias

Fusible Leaf

2½" x 4½"
or fussy cut

Folded Leaves
Medium and Dark
4½" x 5½" of each
or fussy cut

92

Pansy Yardage

Flat Only Trace on smooth side of fusible interfacing. (If making three pansies, trace one extra set.)

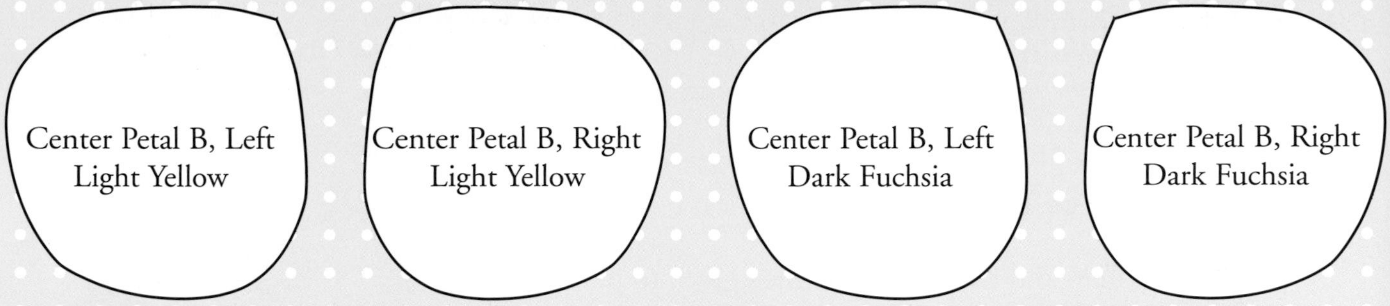

Center Petal B, Left
Light Yellow

Center Petal B, Right
Light Yellow

Center Petal B, Left
Dark Fuchsia

Center Petal B, Right
Dark Fuchsia

Flat and Dimensional Trace on smooth side of fusible interfacing.

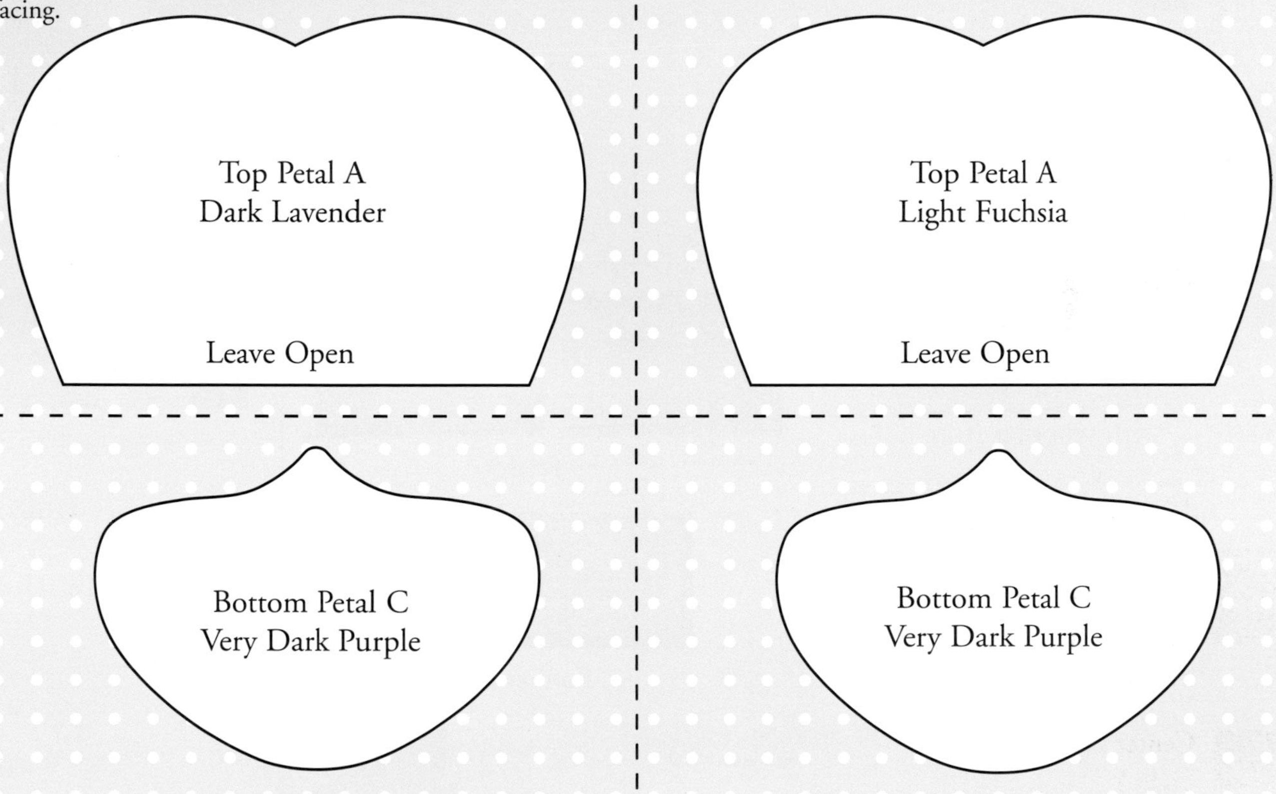

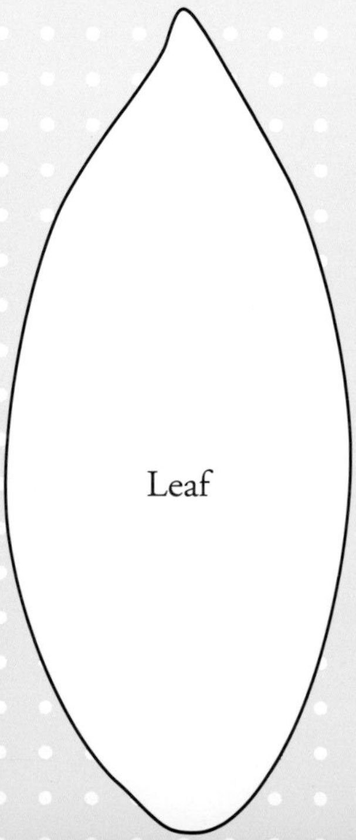

Top Petal A
Dark Lavender

Leave Open

Top Petal A
Light Fuchsia

Leave Open

Bottom Petal C
Very Dark Purple

Bottom Petal C
Very Dark Purple

Flat and Dimensional
Trace on template plastic
and cut out.

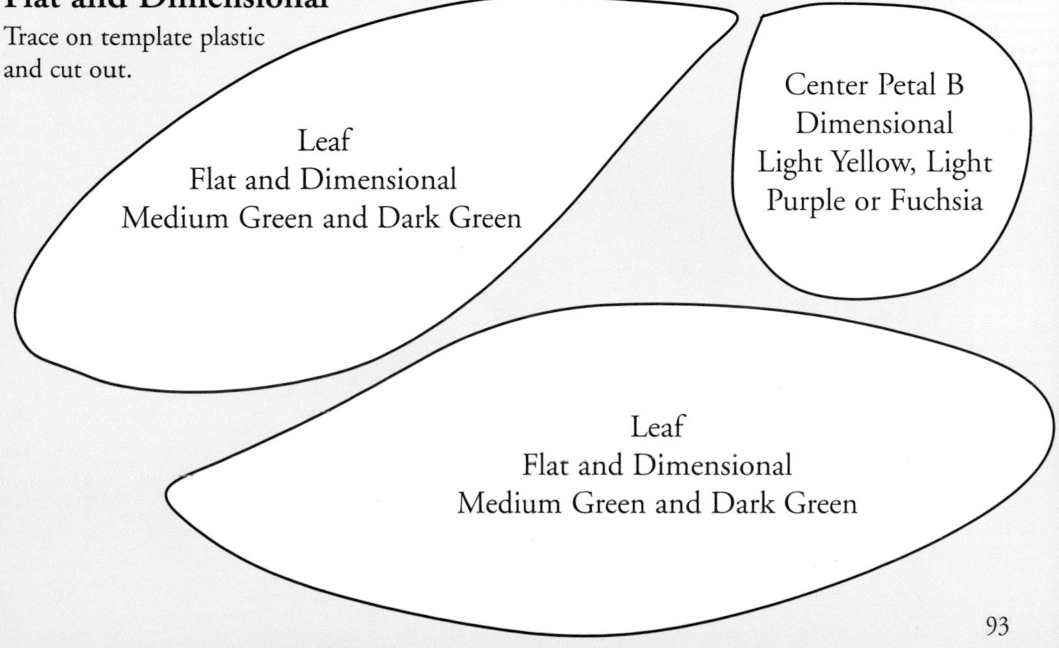

Leaf

Leaf
Flat and Dimensional
Medium Green and Dark Green

Center Petal B
Dimensional
Light Yellow, Light
Purple or Fuchsia

Leaf
Flat and Dimensional
Medium Green and Dark Green

Directions for Flat and Dimensional

If you want three pansies, trace and make all your pieces first and arrange on Handle piece. Use Dimensional picture as your guide. Draw stem after petals are arranged.

1. Place 4½" x 5½" medium and dark greens right sides together. Trace template of each leaf on fabric.

2. Sew on lines and trim. Decide which green to place on top. Cut a small hole on bottom of underneath green. Turn right side out with bodkin and straw.

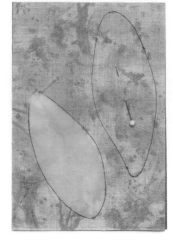

3. Pair right side of fabrics with dotted fusible side of interfacing. Sew, trim, turn, and press with wooded iron.

4. Stuff Petals B and C with cotton batting.

Flat and Dimensional

Top Petal A

Flat Only

Center Petal B

Bottom Petal C

Leaf

5. Sew Handle piece to Basket. Square to 12½".

6. Place Handle piece on placement sheet, arrange Leaves, and fold over tops. Fuse Leaf in place.

Finishing Flat Pansies

1. Make a tuck at center bottom of Petal A. Stitch to hold in place.

2. Arrange Petals and fuse in place.

3. Sew around the outside edges.

4. Sew satin stitch to center of Pansy. Use variegated #5 pearl cotton.
   Patterns are included for two pansies. If making three pansies, trace one extra set.

Making Dimensional Petal B

1. Fold 2½" x 8" fabric in half wrong sides together.

2. Place template on wrong side of fabric. Trace left and right petals.

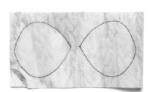

3. Sew on the lines. Trim ⅛" from stitching line. Clip a small opening on back side of petal, and turn right side out. Stuff with cotton batting.

Finishing Dimensional Pansies

1. Make a tuck at center bottom of Petal A. Stitch to hold in place.

2. Place Handle piece on placement sheet, and arrange petals. Fuse in place.

3. Sew around the fused petals and leaves.
   Dimensional: Leave top half of Petal B loose.

4. Sew satin stitch to center of pansy. Use variegated #5 pearl cotton.

Grandmother's garden was an old-fashioned one and held many wild flowers. One of the best loved, because it was one of the earliest to show its colors, was the trillium.

Of course Nancy included it in the flowers she was designing for the quilt club. They were enthusiastic about their basket quilt, and already had more orders than they could fill comfortably for the coming bazaar.

They met once a week. Each member took one special flower for her block contribution. This week it was Nona's turn to contribute her handiwork.

Her trillium was a beautiful shade of red violet. She might have made the petals of red and striped white fast-colored material, but she feared there would scarcely be enough contrast between flower and white background. Mary did use red and white and was delighted with the result.

With pencil, trace Stem line on Handle piece. Press 1¼" x 3" bias stem in half wrong sides together. Place raw edges along inside curve of line. Sew ¼" from raw edge, fold over, and stitch on fold.

Flat

One Petal A
Light Pink
4" x 3"

Two Petals A
Light Pink
4" x 6"

Three Sepals
Dark Green
3½" x 6"

Stem
Green
1¼" x 3" bias

Folded Leaves C, D, & E
Light and Dark Green
4½" x 9" of each

Dimensional

One Petal B
Light Pink
4" x 3"

Two Petals B
Light Pink
4" x 6"

Three Sepals
Dark Green
3½" x 6"

Stem
Green
1¼" x 3" bias

Folded Leaves C, D, & E
Light and Dark Green
4½" x 9" of each

Trillium Yardage

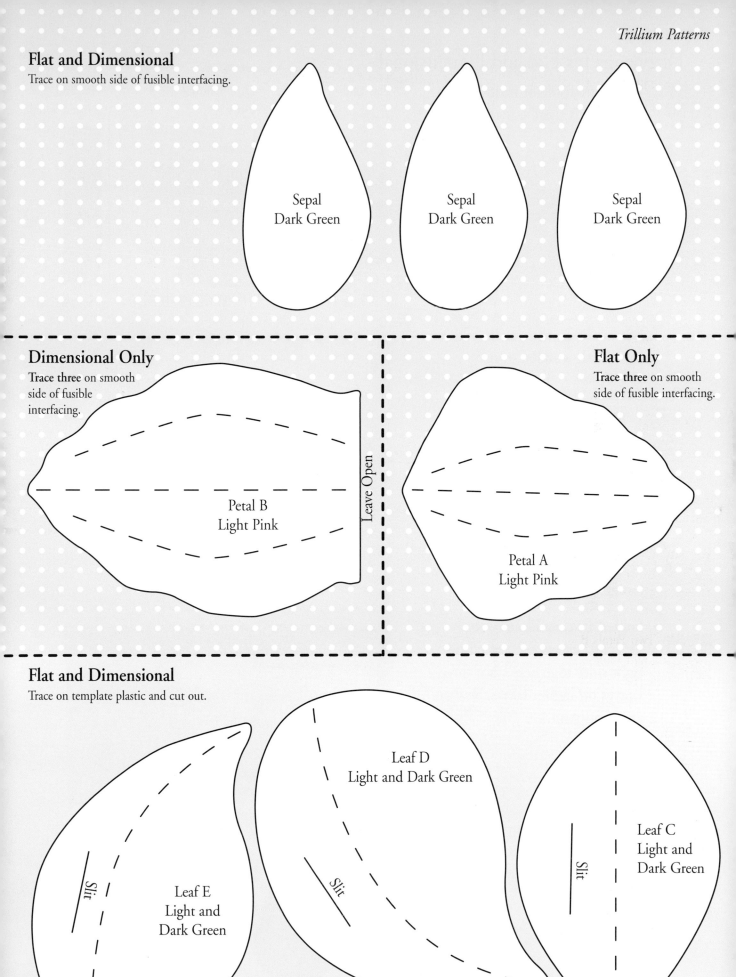

Flat and Dimensional

Trace on smooth side of fusible interfacing.

Sepal
Dark Green

Sepal
Dark Green

Sepal
Dark Green

Dimensional Only

Trace three on smooth side of fusible interfacing.

Petal B
Light Pink

Leave Open

Flat Only

Trace three on smooth side of fusible interfacing.

Petal A
Light Pink

Flat and Dimensional

Trace on template plastic and cut out.

Slit

Leaf E
Light and
Dark Green

Leaf D
Light and Dark Green

Slit

Slit

Leaf C
Light and
Dark Green

Directions for Flat and Dimensional

1. Pair dotted side of fusible inter-facing with right side of fabric.

Flat Only	Dimensional Only	Flat and Dimensional

Three Petals A   Three Petals B   Sepals

2. Sew on lines, trim, turn, and press with wooden iron.

3. Referring to patterns, draw vein lines.
   Flat: Stuff pieces with cotton batting for dimension.
   Dimensional Petal B: Cut batting ½" shorter than fabric and stuff.

Flat Petal A   Dimensional Petal B   Batting for Dimensional B

4. Sew Handle piece to Basket. Square to 12½".

5. **Folded Leaves:** Place two 4½" x 9" pieces of Leaf fabric right sides together. Trace three Leaves on lighter fabric. Sew on lines and trim.

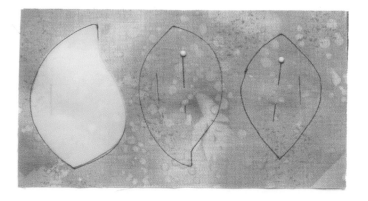

6. Referring to lines on pattern, **slit dark fabric** and turn right side out with bodkin and straw.

7. Place block on placement sheet and position Folded Leaves with light fabric on top. Sew down center of Leaves with machine triple stitch or hand backstitch. Fold dark green sides up, and sew in place.

8. Position Sepals, press in place, and stitch around outside edges.

Finishing the Flat Flower

1. Sew vein lines with triple stitch or backstitch.

2. Position three Petals A on Sepals. Press in place.

3. Sew around the outside edges.

4. Embroider yellow French Knots in center.

Finishing the Dimensional Flower

1. Tuck open end of Petals B in ¼", and finger press. Sew vein lines with triple stitch or backstitch.

2. Double thread a hand sewing needle with matching thread. Stitch along bottom edge, taking long stitches. Assembly-line sew three Petals in a row.

3. Pull tight, closing center. Knot off.

4. Pin Petals on top of Sepals. Sew around outside edges.

5. Embroider yellow French Knots in center.

Bleeding Heart

The eighth flower in the series of Grandmother's Garden quilt was the old, old bleeding heart. Vera said she could remember seeing it in the yard with the snowballs late in May. They all said they liked the air of broken romance and languishing thought which the very name bleeding heart brought forth. As the club discussed the flower they discovered it was a cousin to a much more prosaically named flower—Dutchman's breeches.

"It has another name, too, that I just remembered," said Eleanor. "If you turn the flower upside down and pull it slightly open, it also looks like a lady in the bath."

The ladies laughed at this quaint name for such a pretty flower as they chose their fabrics. The drooping hearts of the flower would be added with embroidery thread after the block was completed.

With pencil, trace vine lines on Handle piece. Cut two 24" pieces of #3 green pearl cotton. By machine, sew a chain stitch. Page 54. By hand, backstitch on the lines.

Flat

Bleeding Heart A
Light Pink
3" x 6"

Dark Pink
3" x 6"

Medium Pink
3" x 6"

Leaves B and C
Dark Green
4" x 5"

Three Leaves D
Green
4" x 5
2½" x 3½"

Dimensional

Bleeding Heart A
Light Pink
3" x 6"

Dark Pink
3" x 6"

Medium Pink
3" x 6"

Leaves B and C
Dark Green
4" x 5"

Three Leaves D
Green
4" x 5"
2½" x 3½"

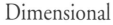

Bleeding Heart Yardage

Flat and Dimensional Trace on smooth side of fusible interfacing.

Bleeding Heart
A
Light Pink

Bleeding Heart
A
Light Pink

Leaf D

Leaf D

Leaf D

Bleeding Heart
A
Medium Pink

Leaf C

Leaf B

Bleeding Heart
A
Medium Pink

Bleeding Heart
A
Dark Pink

Bleeding Heart
A
Dark Pink

Directions for Flat and Dimensional

1. Sew Handle piece to Basket.
   Square to 12½".

2. Place dotted, fusible side of interfacing
   on right side of fabrics.

3. Sew on lines, and trim. Clip bottom
   center on Heart.

4. Turn and press with a wooden iron.

5. Cut cotton batting same size as Bleeding
   Hearts and Leaves, and stuff.

Flat and Dimensional

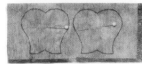

Leaves B and C

Six Hearts A

Three
Leaves D

6. Press Leaves in place, and stitch around
   outside edge.

Sewing Small Hearts by Machine

If your computerized sewing machine
makes hearts, plan Bleeding Heart placement, and make dots for hearts.

1. Sew hearts. Pull threads to back side
   and knot.

2. Triple stitch line from small heart to
   Bleeding Heart.

Making Flat Hearts

1. Fold in half wrong sides together and crease center. Machine edgestitch along center crease.

2. Using the placement sheet as a guide, arrange Hearts on vines.

3. Press in place. Stitch around outside edge.

Making Dimensional Hearts

1. Fold in half wrong sides together, and crease center.

2. Along center crease, machine edgestitch ½" up from bottom.

3. Stuff top part with cotton.

4. Using the placement sheet as a guide, arrange Hearts.

5. Pin in place. Stitch around outside edge.

Sewing Small Hearts by Hand

1. Draw small hearts under Bleeding Hearts.

2. With pink embroidery floss, hand embroider hearts with a satin stitch and connecting line with a back stitch.

Tiger Lily

On the work table in Cornelia's room were pieces of plain fast color gingham in orange, also small pieces of old fashioned calico spotted with tiny bits of carmine or red.

"Oh, I know what we are are making today—tiger lilies."

"Right you are, Nancy, how did you guess?"

"Well, I can remember the showy flower which grandmother kept way back against the stone wall of her garden. It brightened the gray stone even on a sunny day and on a dull day it seemed to burn and glow."

"Of course you know that lilies come in many shades, and have been cultivated since Roman times. It is from the Latin *lilium* that we get the name for this beautiful flower," said Nancy.

The ladies decided that the vivid tiger lily was the best choice for their garden quilt.

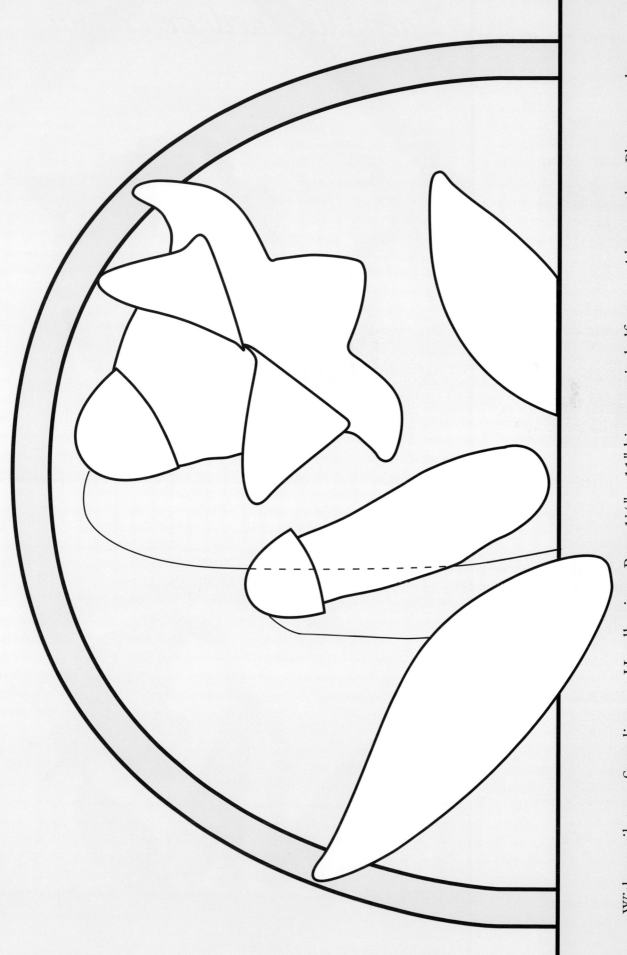

Tiger Lily Position

With pencil, trace Stem lines on Handle piece. Press 1¼" x 11" bias stem in half wrong sides together. Place raw edges along inside curve of line. See page 112.

109

Flat

Lily Petal A
Dark Peach
4½" square

Pieced Bud C
Light and Dark Peach
1" x 3½" of each

Stems and Calyx
Green
1¼" x 11" bias
1½" x 7"

Pieced Leaves
Medium and Dark
1½" x 9" of each

Dimensional

Lily Petal A
Dark Peach
4½" square

Lily Petals B
Light and Dark Peach
4" square of each

Dimensional Bud
Dark Peach
2" x 3½"
Light Peach
1½" x 3½"

Stems and Calyx
Green
1¼" x 11" bias
1½" x 7"

Pieced Leaves
Medium and Dark
1½" x 9" of each

Tiger Lily Yardage

Flat Only
Trace on smooth side of fusible interfacing.

Flat and Dimensional Trace on smooth side of fusible interfacing.

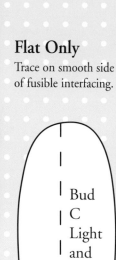

Bud
C
Light
and
Dark
Peach

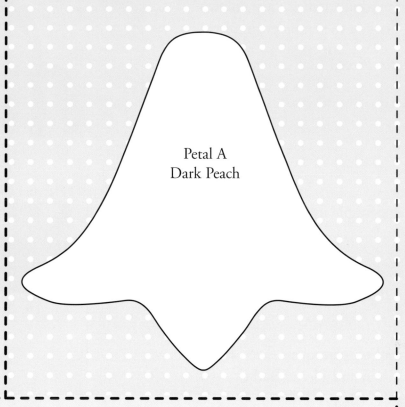

Petal A
Dark Peach

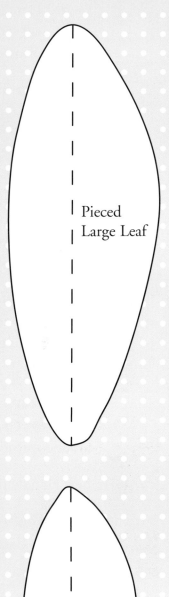

Pieced
Large Leaf

Flat and Dimensional Trace on template plastic and cut out.

Bud Calyx
Dimensional
and Flat

Petal A
Calyx
Flat and
Dimensional

Pieced
Small
Leaf

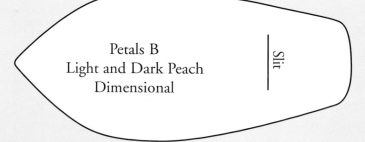

Petals B
Light and Dark Peach
Dimensional

Slit

Directions for Flat and Dimensional

1. Starting from the bottom edge, sew bias stems toward Handle. After stitching around curve, trim strip a half inch beyond stitches. Curl unsewn end, creating a hook at the end. Sew in place.

2. **Flat:** Sew strips for Pieced Bud C together.

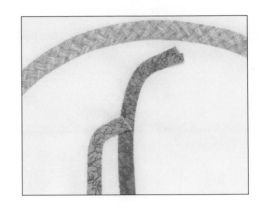

3. Pair dotted side of fusible interfacing with right side of fabric.

4. Sew, trim, turn, and press with wooden iron. Stuff Lily A and Pieced Bud C with cotton batting.

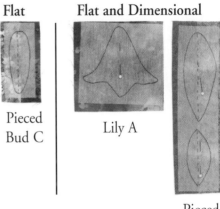

Flat **Flat and Dimensional**

Pieced Bud C

Lily A

Pieced Leaves

5. Place Handle piece on placement sheet. Position Pieced Leaves, Lily A and Pieced Bud C (flat only) on ends of stems. Press in place. Sew around outside edges.

6. Sew Handle piece to Basket. Square to 12½".

7. **Calyx:** Fold 1½" x 7" strip in half right sides together. Trace one of each on fabric.

8. Sew on lines. Trim, and turn right side out with bodkin and small straw.

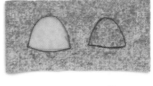

Finishing Flat Lily

1. Pin smaller Calyx on Bud, and larger Calyx on Lily.

2. Machine or hand stitch detail lines with contrasting thread.

3. Embroider French Knots on ends of stitched lines.

Finishing Dimensional Lily

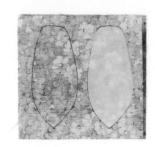

1. **Lily Petal B:** Place 4" light and dark pieces of fabric right sides together. Trace template Petal B twice. Sew on the lines, trim, and slit opening on light fabric as indicated on template. Turn right side out.

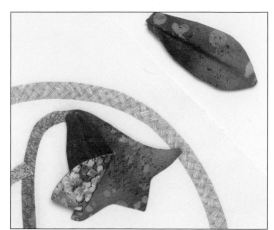

2. Fold in half lengthwise with dark side out, and crease. Unfold and tuck top of petal. Sew tuck.

3. Layer on Lily A with dark side up. Fold back tips of Petal B and pin in place. Stitch. Add Calyx.

4. Optional: Stuff a 2" circle of matching fabric with small cotton ball. Stuff under Petals B.

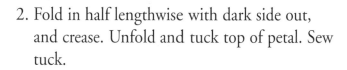

5. **Dimensional Bud:** Sew 3½" sides together, forming a tube. Finger press seam open.

6. Double thread a needle with matching thread. Sew gathering stitch on one end of tube. Pull tight and knot.

7. Turn right side out with bodkin and fat straw.

8. Along top edge, fold two sides in toward center, creating a flat top. Secure with stitches.

9. Place Bud on end of stem. Add Calyx.

10. Embroider French Knots on ends of back stitched lines.

Japanese
Balloon
Flower

W hen the club members entered Edna's home they found gay
balloons floating around. They wondered whether she thought she
was having a children's party, until she explained that the flower for the week was
the balloon flower.

They decided that this flower was
called by its name because the buds
looked just like Japanese lanterns which
open in balloon fashion. They were surprised to learn that deep blue was best
to use for this flower. Nancy made her
flowers and buds of a striped blue and
white fast gingham which was left over
from one of her niece's dresses.

The center of the flower was
embroidered in fast color yellow
embroidery cotton. So were the stamens. In embroidering the center the
satin stitch was used. The outline stitch
which made the stamens was finished
with a French knot.

With pencil, trace Stem lines on Handle piece. Press 1¼" x 8" bias stem in half wrong sides together. Place raw edges along inside curve of line. Sew ¼" from raw edge, fold over, and stitch on fold.

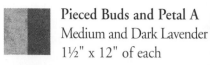

Flat

Pieced Buds and Petal A
Medium and Dark Lavender
1½" x 12" of each

Two Petals B
Dark Lavender
3" x 5"

Center
Light Yellow
2" circle

Leaf
Dark Green
2" x 5"

Pieced Leaf
Medium and Dark
1½" x 4" of each

Stems and Calyx
Green
1¼" x 8" bias
1½" x 7"

Dimensional

Pieced Buds and Three Petals
Medium and Dark
Lavender
3" x 6" of each for buds
2" x 9" of each for petals

Two Petals and Backing
Dark Lavender
2½" x 6"
2½" x 15"

Leaf
Dark Green
2" x 5"

Pieced Leaf
Medium and Dark
1½" x 4" of each

Stems and Calyx
Green
1¼" x 8" bias
1½" x 7"

Japanese Balloon Flower
Yardage

Japanese Balloon Flower Patterns

Flat Only
Trace on smooth side of fusible interfacing.

Petal B
Dark Lavender

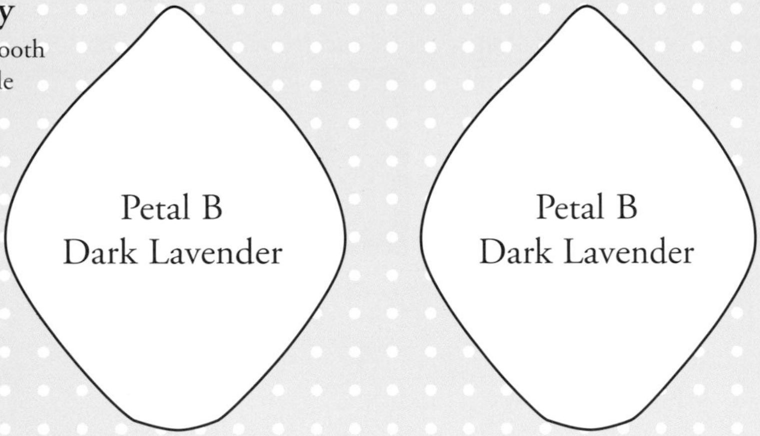

Petal B
Dark Lavender

Petal A
Dark Lavender | Medium Lavender

Flat and Dimensional
Trace on smooth side of fusible interfacing.

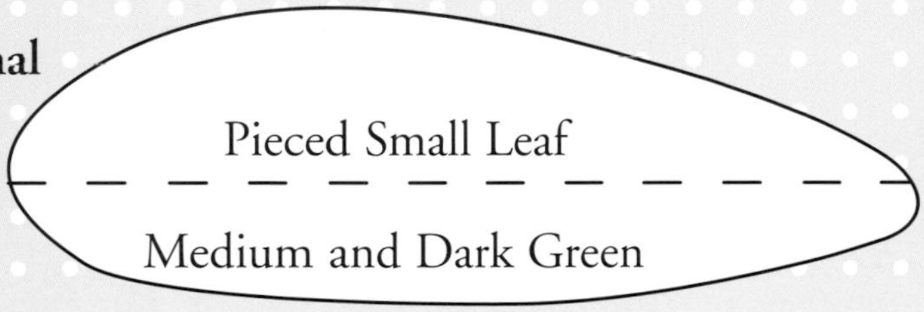

Pieced Small Leaf
Medium and Dark Green

Petal A
Dark Lavender | Medium Lavender

Large Leaf
Dark Green

Petal A
Dark Lavender | Medium Lavender

Flat and Dimensional
Trace on template plastic and cut out.

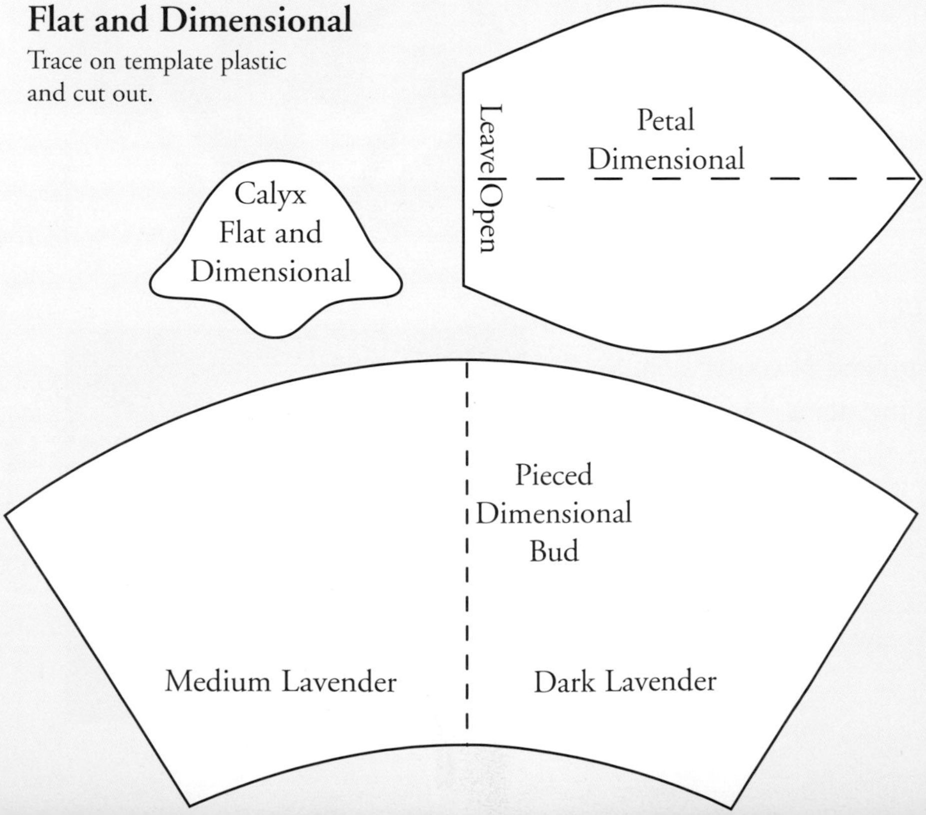

Calyx
Flat and Dimensional

Leave Open

Petal
Dimensional

Dark Lavender | Medium Lavender
Pieced Bud

Pieced
Dimensional
Bud

Medium Lavender | Dark Lavender

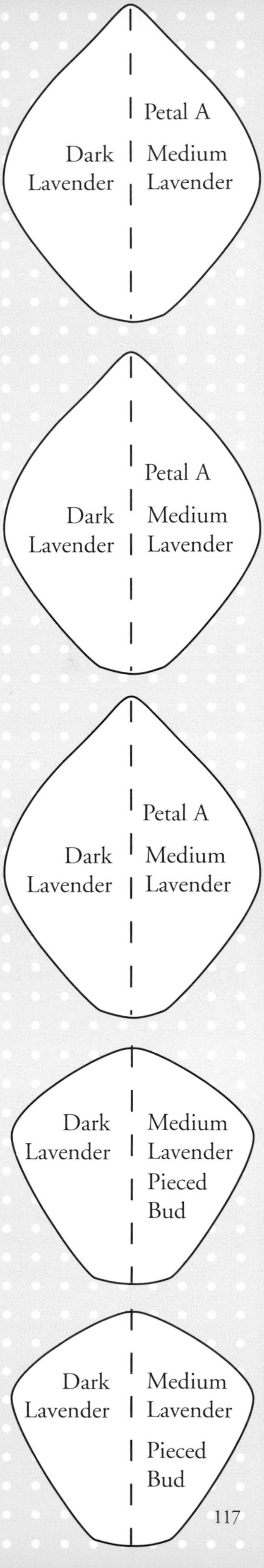

Dark Lavender | Medium Lavender

Pieced Bud

117

Directions for Flat and Dimensional

1. **Flat:** Sew 12" dark and medium lavender strips together. Press seam open.

2. Pair dotted side of fusible interfacing with right side of fabric.

3. Sew, trim, turn, and press with wooden iron. Stuff pieces with cotton batting for dimension.

Flat and Dimensional **Flat Only**

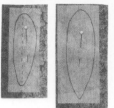

Petal B

Leaves

Pieced
Buds
and
Petal A

4. **Calyx:** Fold 1½" x 7" strip in half right sides together. Trace two Calyx on fabric. Sew on line. Trim, and turn right side out with bodkin and small straw.

5. Place the block on the placement sheet. Position the Leaves. Sew Handle piece to Basket. Square to 12½".

Finishing the Flat Flower

1. Position Petals A and B on end of center stem. Position Buds on remaining stems. Press in place.

2. Pin Calyx on Buds. Sew around the outside edges.

3. Sew 2" circle into yo-yo, and attach to center of Petals.

Making Dimensional Pieced Bud

1. Sew 3" x 6" strips together. Press seam open. Place template's straight line on seam. Trace two Buds on fabric. Cut out.

2. Sew shorter sides together, forming a tube. Finger press seams open.

3. Double thread a needle with matching thread, and sew gathering stitch around wider end of tube. Pull tight and knot off. Turn right side out. Stuff with cotton ball.

4. Flatten bottom edge seams and tack center. Tuck side seams in toward center and flatten. Stitch across flattened center.

Making Dimensional Petals

1. Piece 2" x 9" strips together and trace three Petals on wrong side. Trace two Petals on wrong side of 2½" x 6" strip. Place both pieces right sides together to 2½" x 15" backing strip.

2. Sew on the lines, trim, and turn right side out.

3. Turn raw edges inside and finger press.

4. Double thread a hand sewing needle with matching thread. Stitch along bottom edge, taking long stitches. Assembly-line sew five Petals in a row.

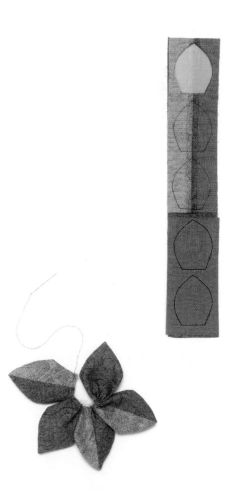

5. Pull tight, closing center. Knot off.

6. Position Petals on end of center stem. Sew to block. Place Buds on ends of remaining stems. Pin Calyx on Buds. Sew around outside edges.

7. Sew 2" circle into yo-yo, and attach to center of Petals, or add French Knots.

Canterbury Bells

W hen the group of the Nancy Page Quilt club were making the blue bells of Scotland for an earlier basket block there had been much talk of another bell flower–the Canterbury bells. They had decided that if that flower came into the pattern they would use pale lavender or pink for these flowers. The real Canterbury flower often comes in a bluish lavender, but they were afraid they might not be able to get that shade in a fast colored gingham.

When they saw the Canterbury bell laid out for them in Belle's home they noticed the merry little fling which the bells had. This had been missing in the blue bells of Scotland. Now that they were more accustomed to appliqueing, they found this easier to do than they would have when they were newer at the job.

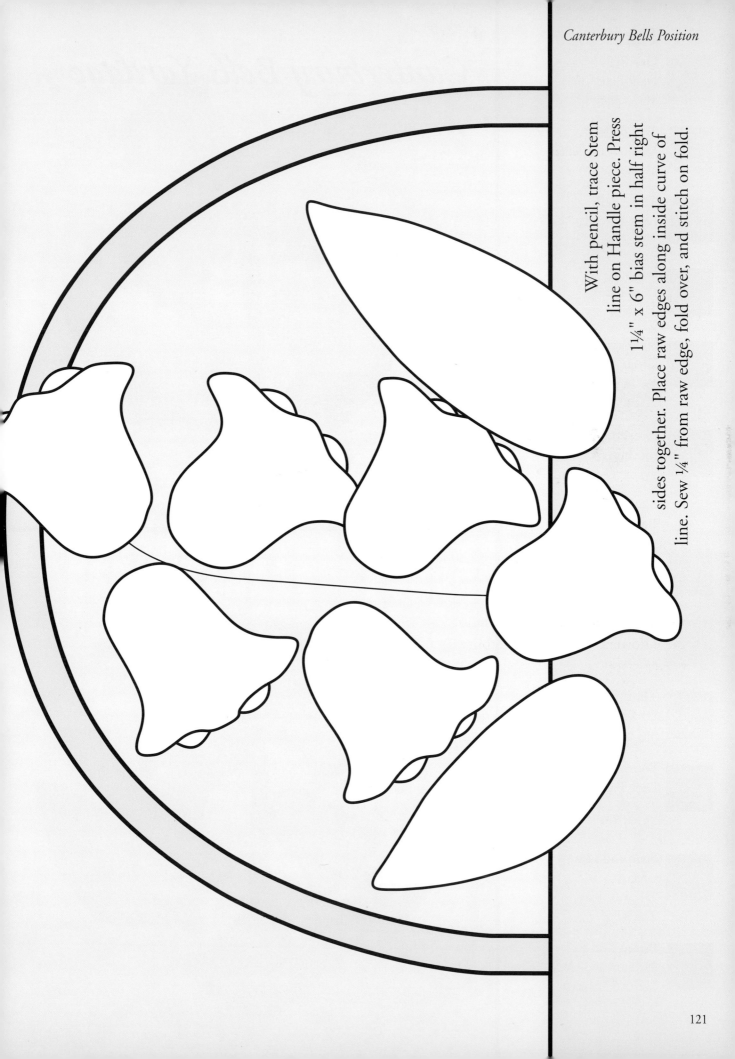

With pencil, trace Stem line on Handle piece. Press 1¼" x 6" bias stem in half right sides together. Place raw edges along inside curve of line. Sew ¼" from raw edge, fold over, and stitch on fold.

Flat

One Bell
Dark Blue
3½" square

Two Bells
Medium Lavender
4½" square

Three Bells
Dark Lavender
3½" x 6½"

Bottoms
Dark Purple
2" x 9"

Stem and Leaf
Green
1¼" x 6" bias
2" x 4"

Pieced Leaf
Medium and Dark
1½" x 5" of each

Dimensional

One Bell
Dark Blue
3½" square

Two Bells
Medium Lavender
4½" square

Three Bells
Dark Lavender
3½" x 6½"

Bottoms and Backing
Dark Purple
2" x 9"
3½" x 15"

Stem and Leaf
Green
1¼" x 6" bias
2" x 4"

Pieced Leaf
Medium and Dark
1½" x 5" of each

Canterbury Bells Yardage

Making Dimensional Bells

1. With template, trace shape on wrong side of three Bell pieces. Line up three pieces right sides together to 3½" x 15" dark backing. Cut strip in three pieces.

2. Sew on lines and trim.

3. Clip opening in upper half of dark side. Turn right side out. Stuff with cotton batting.

4. With a double strand of matching thread, run gathering stitch along dotted line as indicated on pattern.

6. Gather lightly and round out bell shape.

7. Pin Bells in place and stitch following arrows.

Stuffing Dimensional Bells (Optional)

1. Cut six 2" circles of dark purple fabric. With double strand of thread, sew around 2" circle with long running stitches. Stuff with small cotton ball. Pull tightly and knot. Do not cut threads.

2. Insert needle through opening in Bell and stitch through background, catching cotton ball inside Bell. Knot.

3. Sew French Knots at bottom of Bells.

A t Susan's house, the ladies arrived to see a festive display of streamers and banners printed with stars and comets, and a picnic table set with a variety of summer treats and lemonade.

"Can it be Fourth of July already?" they asked.

"No," said Susan, laughing. "I thought this would be a good way to introduce our next flower, the shooting star. Since it blooms in summer fields, I decided to have a picnic lunch to celebrate it."

"The petals of the shooting star are reddish lavender and the anthers on the stamens are a rich gold. They are so shaped that they give the effect of a golden cone or center," said Nancy. "I think this must be where it got its name, like a shooting star burning across the heavens."

"Each flower has five petals, all cut from the same pattern. But some of the petals overlap so that the finished effect is not monotonous. We will finish our shooting stars with French knots in gold embroidery thread."

With pencil, trace Stem lines on Handle piece. Press 1¼" x 11" bias stem in half wrong sides together. Place raw edges along inside curve of line. See page 130.

Flat

Top Petals
Light Fuchsia
Three 1½" x 2½"

Bottom Petals
Medium Fuchsia
Six 1½" x 2½"

Stems
Green
1¼" x 11" bias

Pieced Leaves
Light and Medium
1¾" x 9" each

Dimensional

One Flower
Medium Purple
One 3½" square

Two Flowers
Medium Fuchsia
Two 3½" squares

Backing
Light Yellow
Three 3½" squares

Stems
Green
1¼" x 11" bias

Pieced Leaves
Light and Medium
1¾" x 9" each

128

Shooting Star Yardage

Flat Only
Trace onto fusible
interfacing.

Flat and Dimensional
Trace onto fusible interfacing.

Top Petal
Light Fuchsia

Top Petal
Light Fuchsia

Top Petal
Light Fuchsia

Medium
Green

Light
Green

Pieced
Leaf

Bottom Petal
Medium
Fuchsia

Bottom Petal
Medium
Fuchsia

Bottom Petal
Medium
Fuchsia

Bottom Petal
Medium
Fuchsia

Bottom Petal
Medium
Fuchsia

Bottom Petal
Medium
Fuchsia

Medium
Green

Light
Green

Pieced
Leaf

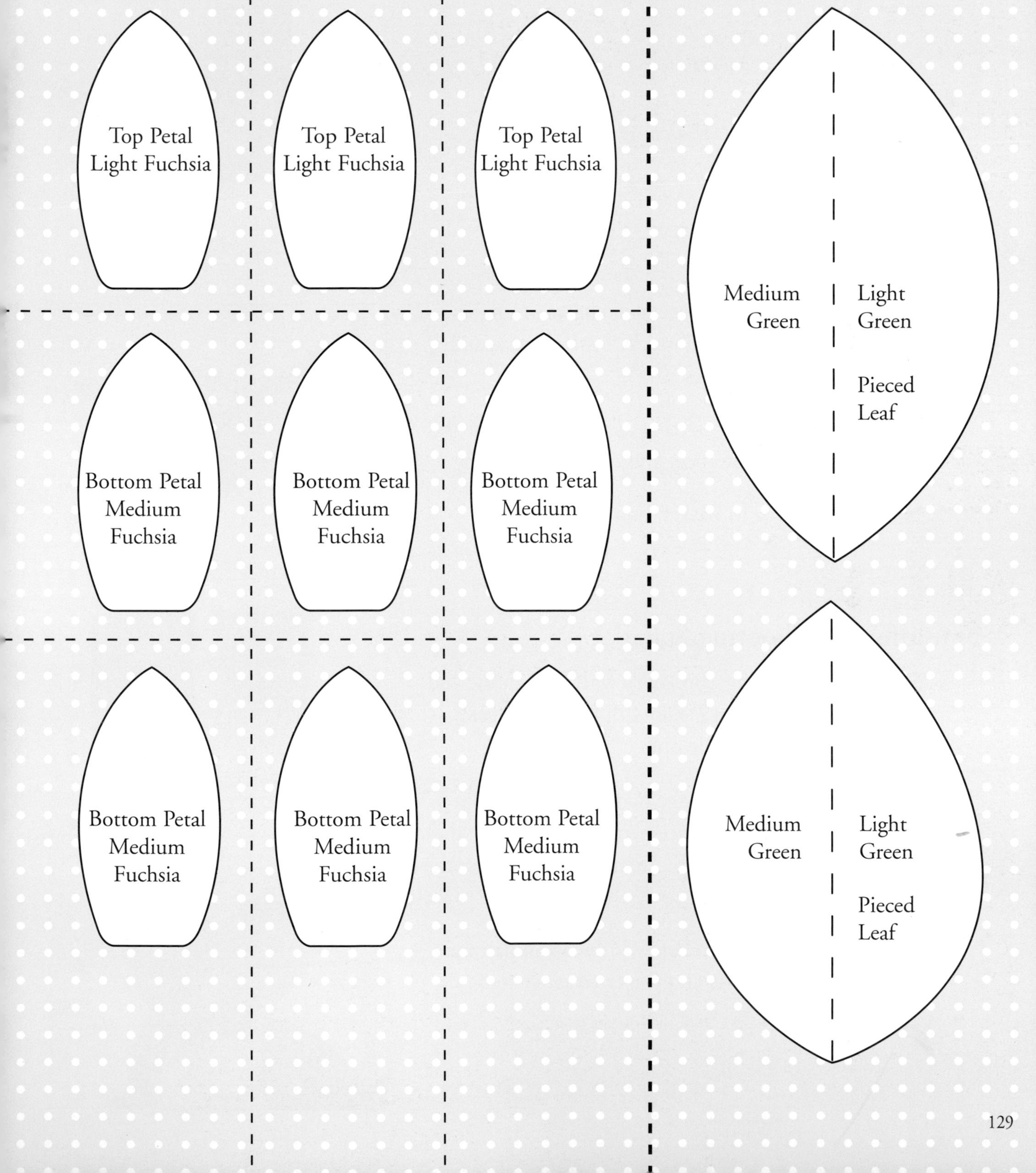

Directions for Flat and Dimensional

1. Sew 1¾" x 9" leaf strips right sides together. Press seam open.

2. Place right side of sewn leaf strips with dotted fusible side of interfacing. Sew on lines, trim, and turn right side out.

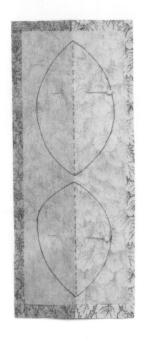

3. Place Handle piece on placement sheet. Arrange leaves with light fabric to inside. Fuse in place and sew around outside edges.

4. Sew stems in place by starting at the top. Stop at the curve, clip seam allowance, and continue stitching.

5. Sew Handle piece to Basket. Square to 12½".

Finishing Flat Shooting Star

1. Sew three interfacing Top Petals with light fabric and six interfacing Bottom Petals with medium fabrics. Trim, and turn right side out.

2. To make one flower, arrange two medium Bottom Petals according to the placement sheet. Overlap the two Petals at the bottom. Fuse in place and finish the outside edges.

3. Stuff the three light Top Petals with cotton batting. Fold in half lengthwise and finger crease center.

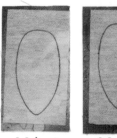

Make 3   Make 6

4. Pin the Top Petal in place on the Bottom Petals. For added dimension, pinch in the bottom of the petal to make it raise slightly. Finish the outside edges.

5. Sew French knots and satin stitch pistil to bottom of flowers.

Finishing Dimensional Shooting Star

1. Place three 3½" yellow squares right sides together with pink and purple squares. Stitch ¼" seam around outside edge. Clip corners and trim seams to ⅛". Cut openings in center of yellow fabric and turn right sides out.

2. Press. Fold in fourths and press crease lines.

3. Double thread a hand sewing needle with matching pink or purple thread. The dashed lines indicate the sewing line. Beginning at the arrow, stitch an arc through the first quarter square. Pull tight and wrap the thread around the outside edge two times to secure the gathers.

4. Continue stitching an arc through each quarter square, forming four petals. Knot off.

5. Position the flower with the yellow side underneath. Beginning at the outside tip, roll one petal tightly to the center, exposing the yellow underside. Tack roll in back and stitch in place.

6. Using the placement sheet as a guide, arrange and pin flowers on Handle. Sew outside edges. Satin stitch pistil to bottom of flowers.

Jonquil

W hen the ladies gathered again, they were excitedly discussing which flower might be next.

"I hope it will be a violet," said Claire, "that's my favorite flower!"

Hyacinths and carnations were all suggested, and had their champions, but Nancy shook her head as she brought out a fabric of deep yellow and gold.

"Now if it was a violet or a carnation, we couldn't use this, could we? Our flower for this week is the jonquil, sometimes called the daffodil. The name jonquil comes from the Spanish word *jonquillo*, or rush, and refers to the rush-like leaves."

"Jonquils are the prettiest of the springtime blooms," sighed Claire. "I don't mind not having violets after all."

With pencil, trace Stem line on Handle piece. Press 1¼" x 5" bias stem in half wrong sides together. Place raw edges along inside curve of line. Sew ¼" from raw edge, fold over, and stitch on fold.

Flat

Base A
Medium Yellow
4½" square

Petal E
Light Yellow
3" x 6"

Center
Dark Yellow
2½" square

Stem
Green
1¼" x 5" bias

Leaves
Light Green
Two 2" x 6"
Dark Green
Two 2" x 6"

Dimensional

Base A
Medium Yellow
4½" square

Petal F
Light Yellow
3" x 16"

Center
Dark Yellow
2½" x 3½"

Stem
Green
1¼" x 5" bias

Leaves
Light Green
Two 2" x 6"
Dark Green
Two 2" x 6"

Jonquil Yardage

Flat Only

Trace on smooth side of fusible interfacing.

Center
Dark Yellow

Flat and Dimensional

Trace on smooth side of fusible interfacing.

Base A
Medium Yellow

Petal E
Light Yellow

Petal E
Light Yellow

Petal E
Light Yellow

Leaf B

Leaf C

Flat and Dimensional

Trace on template plastic and cut out.

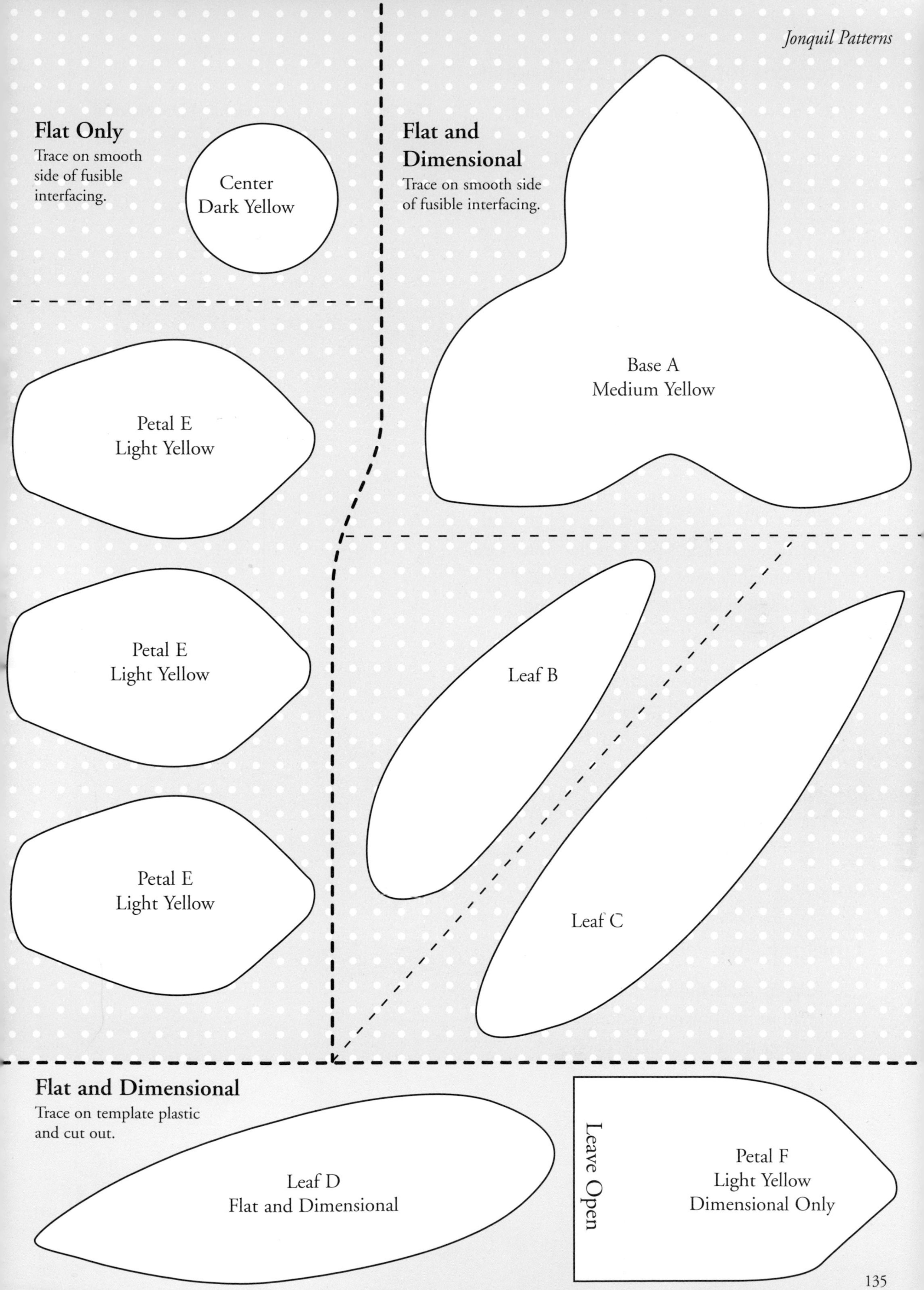

Leaf D
Flat and Dimensional

Leave Open

Petal F
Light Yellow
Dimensional Only

Directions for Flat and Dimensional

1. Pair dotted side of fusible interfacing with right side of fabric.

2. Sew on lines, clip inside curves, turn, and press with wooden iron. Stuff E Petals and Center.

Flat Only

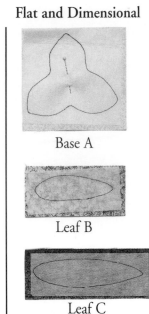

Petal E

Center

Flat and Dimensional

Base A

Leaf B

Leaf C

Leaf D

3. **Leaf D**: Place 2" x 6" pieces of light and dark green right sides together. Trace Leaf D on fabric. Sew on line, trim, cut a small hole near bottom on light side, and turn.

4. Referring to placement sheet, position fusible pieces and press in place. Position Leaf D, and fold over top. Sew around outside edges.

5. Sew Handle piece to Basket. Square block to 12½".

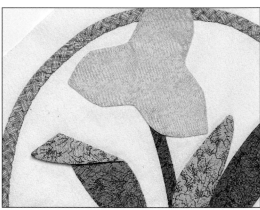

Finishing Flat Petals E and Center

1. Layer Petals and Center on Base, and press in place. Optional: Make yo-yo center from 2½" circle.

2. Sew around outside edges.

Making Dimensional Petals

1. Fold 3" x 16" light yellow strip right sides together lengthwise. Trace three Petals F on strip, lining up "open edge" with edge of fabric. Allow ½" between Petals. Pin. Stitch on drawn lines.

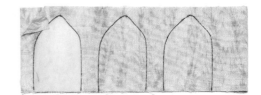

2. Trim seam to ⅛" and turn right side out. Press edges. Cut cotton batting ½" shorter and stuff. Turn raw edge under a ¼" and finger press.

3. Double thread a hand sewing needle with matching thread and knot. Stitch along bottom edge, taking long stitches. Assembly-line sew three Petals in a row. Pull tight and knot off.

4. Center Petals on Base and pin. Stitch in place.

Making Dimensional Center

1. Fold 2½" x 3½" strip of dark yellow in half widthwise. Stitch seam on 2½" side, and backstitch at each end. Fingerpress seam open.

2. Turn top half of tube right side out, using your finger or pencil eraser to help form shape.

3. Hand stitch a long gathering stitch around bottom raw edges. Pull tight and knot, forming a small cap shape. Leave thread attached. Roll the folded edge over the outside of cap.

4. Place in center of Jonquil, and hand stitch in place with attached thread.

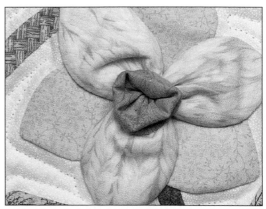

Bluet

"Oh goody, I am so glad we are going to use more blue in this quilt. I had some pieces left over from the blue bells of Scotland and I did want to have another patch of blue in my flower quilt."

"Well, of course, we could not have grandmother's garden without the forget-me-not. To tell the truth, though, I am using the bluet today which is easier to applique and which is often mistakenly called the forget-me-not."

"The Bluet is really a Quaker lady, sometimes called an Innocent, but under any name whatever it is a dainty little flower."

While they worked Esther told of the legend which called these flowers the symbol of peace and prosperity if only one will be content with his lot. Like the bluebird, the bluet signifies contentment and happiness at home. Longfellow called the blue and gold flowers the stars of the earth since the stars in heaven are the forget-me-nots of the angels.

With pencil, trace Stem lines on Handle piece. Press 1¼" x 11" bias stem in half right sides together. Place raw edges along inside curve of line. Sew ¼" from raw edge, fold over, and stitch on fold.

Flat

Folded Flower A
Light and Dark Blue
3½" square of each

Flower B
Light and Medium Blue
3½" square of each

Center
Light Yellow
Two 2" circles

Leaves
Light and Dark
2" x 11" of each

Stems
Green
1¼" x 11" bias

Dimensional

Folded Flower A
Light and Dark Blue
3½" square of each

Flower C
Light and Medium Blue
3½" square of each

Leaves
Light and Dark
2" x 11" of each

Stems
Green
1¼" x 11" bias

Bluet Yardage

Flat Only
Trace two on fusible interfacing.

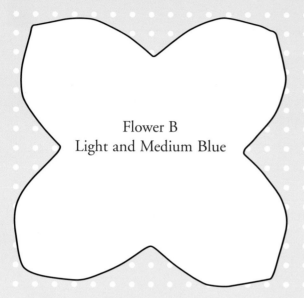

Flower B
Light and Medium Blue

Dimensional Only
Trace two on fusible interfacing. Trace circle.

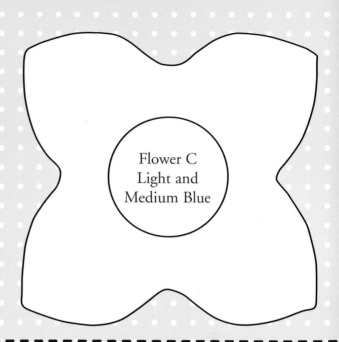

Flower C
Light and
Medium Blue

Flat and Dimensional
Trace on template plastic and cut out.

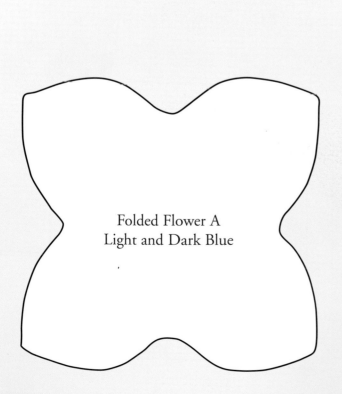

Folded Flower A
Light and Dark Blue

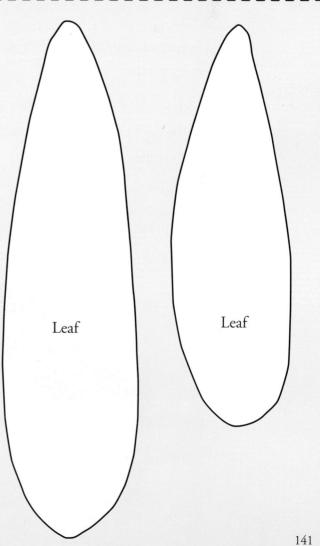

Leaf

Leaf

Directions for Flat and Dimensional

1. Place 2" x 11" light green and dark green right sides together. Trace one template of each leaf on fabric. Sew on lines and trim. Cut a small hole on wrong side of light green near bottom. Turn right side out with bodkin and straw.

2. Fold over tops of leaves. Position on Handle piece. Sew in place.

3. Sew Handle piece to Basket. Square to 12½".

4. **Folded Flower:** Place 3½" light and dark squares right sides together. Trace A on wrong side of light.

5. Sew on lines and trim. Clip inside curves. Cut a small hole in center of light. Turn right side out. Refer to numbered Petals in next steps.

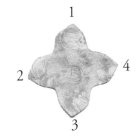

6. Position Flower A with light side up. Starting on left side, fold up dark petals #2 and #3 diagonally.

7. Fold right petal #4 up on diagonal. Center petal #3 extends in front.

8. Push center petal #3 flat.

With pencil, trace Stem lines on Handle piece. Press 1¼" x 6" bias stem in half wrong sides together. Place raw edges along inside curve of line. Sew ¼" from raw edge, fold over, and stitch on fold.

Flat

Flower A
Medium Fuchsia
4" square

Bud and B Top
Medium Purple
2" x 3"
2½" x 4"

B Bottom
Light Purple
2" x 3"

Stems and Calyx
Green
1¼" x 6" bias
1½" x 2"
1½" x 3"

Leaves
Medium Green
5" x 7"

Dimensional

Flower A
Medium Fuchsia
4" square

Bud and B Top
Medium Purple
3" square
2½" x 4"

B Bottom
Light and Medium Purple
4½" square each

Stems and Calyx
Green
1¼" x 6" bias
1½" x 8"

Leaves
Medium Green
5" x 7"

Morning Glory Yardage

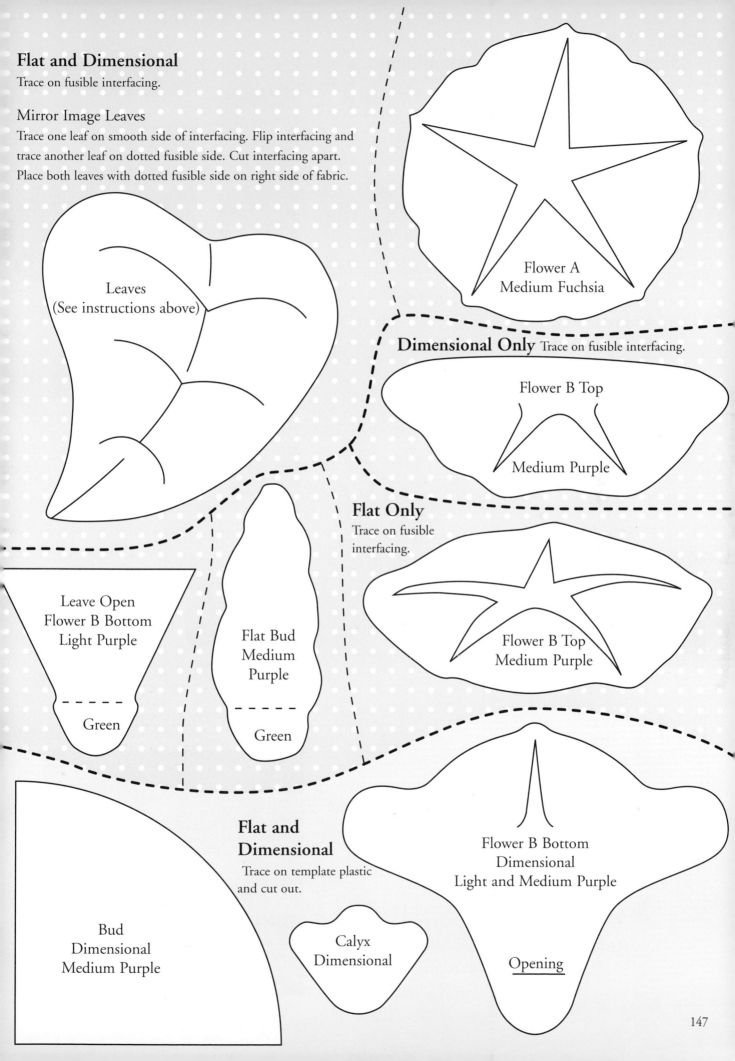

Flat and Dimensional

Trace on fusible interfacing.

Mirror Image Leaves

Trace one leaf on smooth side of interfacing. Flip interfacing and trace another leaf on dotted fusible side. Cut interfacing apart. Place both leaves with dotted fusible side on right side of fabric.

Leaves
(See instructions above)

Flower A
Medium Fuchsia

Dimensional Only Trace on fusible interfacing.

Flower B Top

Medium Purple

Flat Only
Trace on fusible interfacing.

Leave Open
Flower B Bottom
Light Purple

Green

Flat Bud
Medium
Purple

Green

Flower B Top
Medium Purple

Flat and Dimensional

Trace on template plastic and cut out.

Bud
Dimensional
Medium Purple

Calyx
Dimensional

Flower B Bottom
Dimensional
Light and Medium Purple

Opening

147

Directions for Flat and Dimensional

1. **Flat Only:** Sew Calyx 1½" green strips to Bud and Flower B Bottom.

2. **Flat and Dimensional:** Pair dotted side of marked fusible interfacing with right side of corresponding fabric.

Flat and Dimensional **Dimensional**

Two Leaves

Flower B Top

Flower A

3. Sew, trim, turn, and press with wooden iron.

Flat Only

4. Referring to patterns, draw vein lines on right side of pieces. Stuff pieces with cotton batting for dimension.

5. Sew on vein lines. If stitching by machine, choose a triple stitch. If stitching by hand, backstitch with pearl cotton. Make large yellow French knot in center. With two strands of white embroidery floss, make lines radiating from center knot.

6. Sew Handle piece to Basket. Square to 12½".

7. Referring to placement sheet, fuse pieces in place. Stitch around outside edges.

Finishing Dimensional Flowers

1. **Calyx:** Fold 1½" x 8" strip right sides together. Trace two templates on wrong side of fabric, sew on lines, trim, turn, and press.

2. **Flower B Bottom:** Place 4½" squares right sides together. Trace Bottom template on wrong side of fabric, sew on lines, and trim. Cut slit on dark fabric near bottom and turn right side out with bodkin and straw. At top of dark side, sew vein lines.

3. With light side up, place Bottom B on Top B. Roll over top and match sides. Pin in place, rounding out into bell shape. Stitch sides and bottom in place. Sew Calyx.

4. **Bud:** Line up Bud template on 3" square. Trace curve, and cut on line. Fold in half right sides together, and stitch.

5. Turn right side out. With hand sewing needle, gather curved edge, pull tight, and knot.

6. Holding pointed end, twist gathered end counterclockwise. Wrap Calyx around gathered end, and pin to background. Sew in place.

Finishing Flat and Dimensional with Tendrils

Use the hand couching stitch.

1. Thread a large-eyed needle with green #3 pearl cotton. Knot.

2. From wrong side of block, bring needle up near stem. Following lines on pattern, make several loops with pearl cotton, and pin loops in place.

3. Thread a hand sewing needle with matching thread. Every ¼", take a tiny stitch across pearl cotton. Pull large needle to wrong side and knot.

The Nancy Page quilt club met at Nancy's for the next to the last block. Her home was a riot of color for there were pots of tulips everywhere and that gave the members the clue for the day.

"Of course, our flower is the tulip."

On the table were bits of yellow, orange, deep red, lavender, purple, and striped pink and white.

"You guessed right. It is the tulip–and since tulips are such gorgeous affairs I am giving you a wide choice in colors. Take whatever you want. I suggest that you make all three tulips of different colored material. These are all fast colors, and of about the same weight. You are safe in any choice you may make."

They talked about the tulip craze in Holland years ago and the various stories and legends attached to the flowers. They spoke of the fortunes made by tulip growers in those far off days. The block was one of the gayest and one of the prettiest thus far.

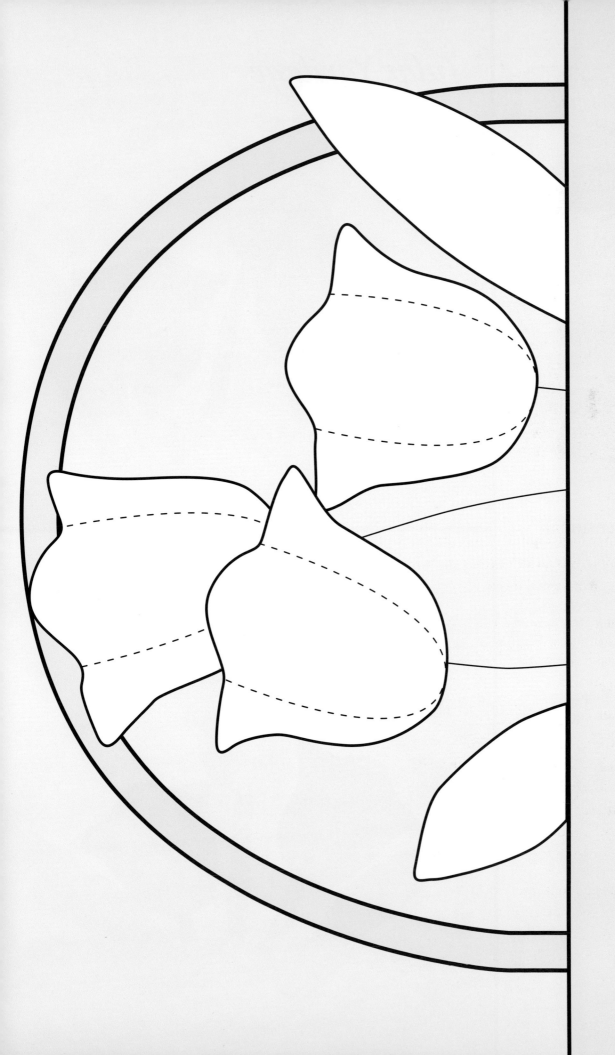

With pencil, trace Stem lines on Handle piece. Press 1¼" x 10" bias stem in half wrong sides together. Place raw edges along inside curve of line. Sew ¼" from raw edge, fold over, and stitch on fold.

Flat

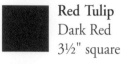
Yellow Tulip
Dark Yellow
3½" square

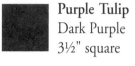
Red Tulip
Dark Red
3½" square

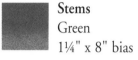
Purple Tulip
Dark Purple
3½" square

Stems
Green
1¼" x 8" bias

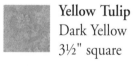
Leaves
Green
2" x 10"

Dimensional

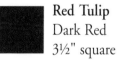
Yellow Tulip
Dark Yellow
3½" square

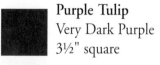
Red Tulip
Dark Red
3½" square

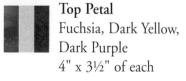
Purple Tulip
Very Dark Purple
3½" square

Top Petal
Fuchsia, Dark Yellow,
Dark Purple
4" x 3½" of each

Stems
Green
1¼" x 8" bias

Leaves
Green
2" x 10"

Tulip Yardage

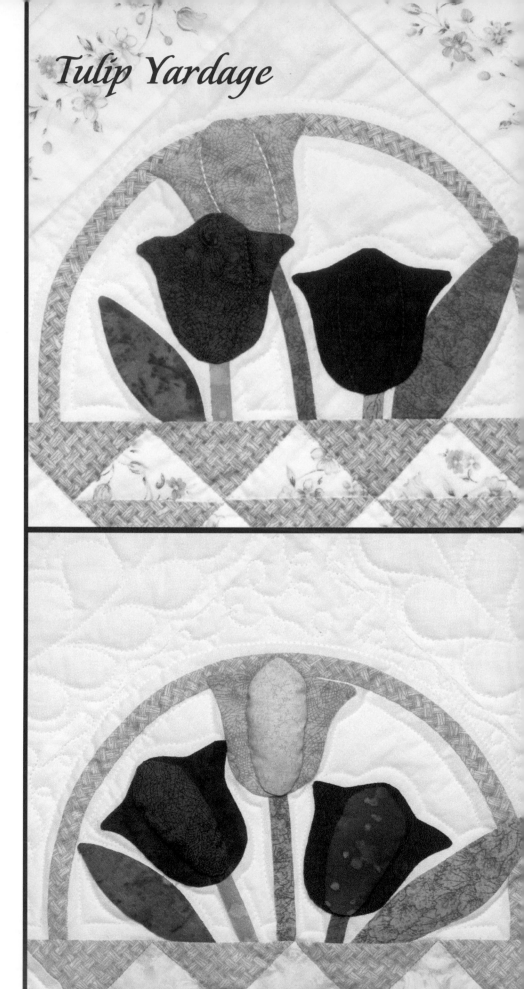

**Flat and
Dimensional**

Trace on template plastic
and cut out.

Flat and Dimensional

Trace on right side of
fusible interfacing.

Dimensional
Template

Top Petal

Leaf

Tulip
Dark Yellow

Tulip
Dark Red

Flat Template

Top Petal

Leaf

Tulip
Dark Purple

153

Directions for Flat and Dimensional

1. Trace Stem lines on Handle piece, and sew in place.

2. Trace Top Petal templates for Flat or Dimensional on template plastic, and cut out.

3. Trace three Tulips and two Leaves on fusible interfacing. Cut apart.

4. Pair right side of fabrics with dotted fusible side of interfacing patterns. Sew on lines, trim, and turn right side out. Stuff with cotton batting.

Flat and Dimensional

5. Place Handle piece on placement sheet. Overlap and arrange Tulips.

6. Fuse pieces in place, and sew around the outside edges.

7. Sew Handle piece to Basket. Square to 12½".

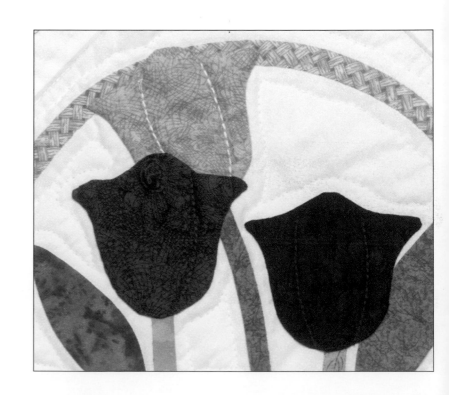

Finishing Flat Tulips

1. Place Top Petal template on Tulip. Lightly pencil outline.

2. Sew outline with stitch on sewing machine as Triple Stitch or Top Stitch, or hand outline stitch.

Finishing Dimensional Tulips

1. Fold 4" x 3½" piece in half with right sides together.

2. Trace template on wrong side. Sew on the lines.

3. Clip small hole on bottom of inside. Turn right side out. Stuff with cotton batting.

4. Place on Tulip, and pin in place by gently pushing sides in toward center.

5. Handstitch sides and bottom.

6. Place cotton batting behind Top Petal.

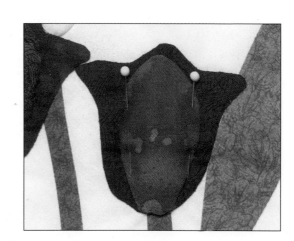

Zinnia

B oth the tulip block of last week and the zinnia of this week have been cho-
sen for dual purposes. No grandmother's garden would be complete without
these two flowers and since they come in such varied colors, the quilt club members had a chance to use up scraps of cloth left from other flowers. The zinnia of
grandmother's day was little more than a weed, but today they are large full-fash-
ioned and gorgeous in their colorings. Tawny oranges, dulled purples, rose which
has been grayed to a richness of dying embers, are some of the colors in the zinnias of today. The club members decided to
make the flowers using three tones of the same
color in each flower.

The club realized that this was the last
flower of the quilt. They had 16 flowers, not
counting the rose. That was to be repeated
three times and put at each end of four corner
blocks, making 20 blocks or baskets in all.

With pencil, trace Stem line on Handle piece. Press 1¼" x 5" bias stem in half wrong sides together. Place raw edges along inside curve of line. Sew ¼" from raw edge, fold over, and stitch on fold.

Flat

Petal C and Bud F
Dark Purple
5" x 6"

Petal D
Medium Purple
4" Square

Petal E and G
Light Purple
5" Square

Leaf A
Light and Medium Green
2½" x 8" of each

Leaf B, Calyx and Stem
Dark Green
3½" x 4"
1¼" x 5" bias

Dimensional

Petal C and Bud F
Dark Purple
5" x 6"

Petal D
Medium Purple
4" Square

Ruched Flower and G
Light Purple
2" x 4"
1¼" x 20"

Ruched Flower
Medium Lavender
1¼" x 20"

Leaf A
Light and Medium Green
2½" x 8" of each

Leaf B, Calyx and Stem
Dark Green
3½" x 4"
1¼" x 5" bias

Zinnia Yardage

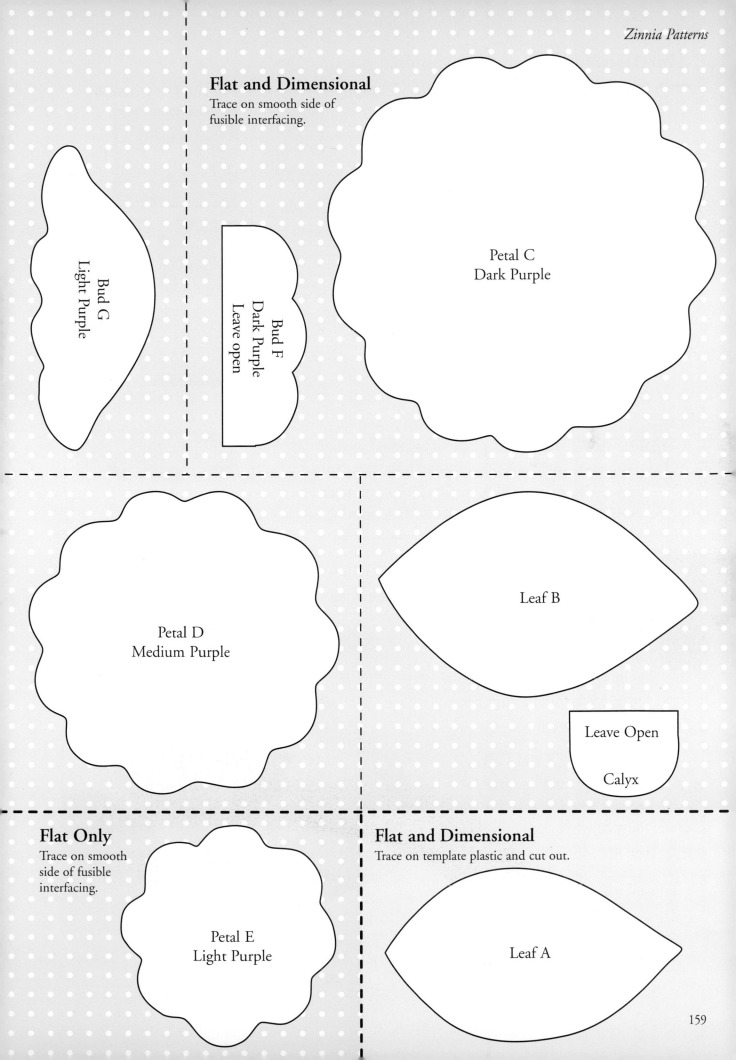

Flat and Dimensional
Trace on smooth side of
fusible interfacing.

Bud G
Light Purple

Bud F
Dark Purple
Leave open

Petal C
Dark Purple

Petal D
Medium Purple

Leaf B

Leave Open

Calyx

Flat Only
Trace on smooth
side of fusible
interfacing.

Petal E
Light Purple

Flat and Dimensional
Trace on template plastic and cut out.

Leaf A

Directions for Flat and Dimensional

1. Sew Handle piece to Basket. Square to 12½".

2. Pair dotted side of fusible interfacing with right side of fabric.

Flat Only

Petal E

Flat and Dimensional

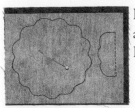

Petal C and Bud F

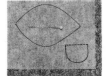

Petal D and Bud G

Leaf B and Calyx

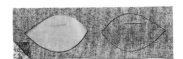

Leaf A

3. **Leaf A:** Place 2½" x 8" pieces of light and medium green fabric right sides together with medium fabric on top. Trace one Leaf A on fabric, flip, and trace second Leaf in opposite direction. Mark opening as indicated by slit on medium fabric.

4. Sew, trim and clip inside curves. Turn, and press with wooden iron. Stuff E and G with cotton batting.

5. Place block on placement sheet. Position Leaves A with light side up. Fold up medium edge. Layer Zinnia with Petal C on the bottom.

6. Position Bud F and Calyx. Press in place. Place Bud G on top. Press, and finish outside edges.

Making Dimensional Center

This technique is referred to as Ruching.

1. Fold edges of 1¼" x 20" strip to center, wrong sides together. Press.

2. Place folded raw edges underneath. Along top edge, begin 1" from right end, and make small dots on the edges every 1". Along bottom edge, begin ½" from edge and make small dots every 1".

3. Thread a hand sewing needle with a 24" double strand of matching thread, and knot. Be sure to wax your thread.
Starting at the right end of the strip, stitch running stitches from dot to dot in zig zag direction. Loop the thread over the folded edge each time you change direction. Stitch several inches and pull, gathering the fabric on both sides.

4. Stitch to the end, gathering to 10" or half the original length. Adjust the fabric petals and knot.

5. To form the center, baste across the bottom of the first six petals, pull into a circle, and tack together. Arrange seventh petal under the first, and continue to spiral around the center. Continuously stitch as you arrange. Tuck the end underneath the flower, and knot off.

6. Hand or machine sew the ruching to the center of the Zinnia.

Quilt with Solid Square Setting

Cut the pieces for the Side Triangles, Corner Triangles, and Solid Squares from the Solid Square fabric listed on the Yardage Chart. The largest pieces are cut first.

Side Triangles

1. Cut 18¼" strips, using the 6" x 24" ruler and gridded cutting mat. Cut strips into 18¼" squares. Excess fabric can be used for Corner Triangles and Solid Squares.

	18¼" strip	into	Squares
Baby	1		1
Lap	1		2
Twin	2		3
Double	2		4
Queen	2		4
King	2		4

2. Line up yardstick or two rulers on diagonal and draw a line. Line up on second diagonal and draw a second line. Staystitch on both sides of diagonal line.

3. Cut into fourths on both diagonals with the rotary cutter and two rulers placed end to end. These diagonal cuts are on the bias. Handle carefully so bias does not stretch. When Side Triangles are sewn into quilt, the bias is on the inside, and the straight-of-grain is on the outside edge of quilt.

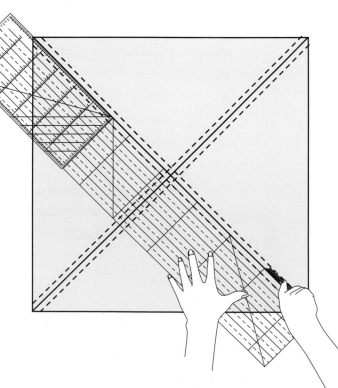

Solid Squares

Solid Squares are the same size as your 12½" Basket blocks. If it was necessary to square your Basket to a different size, such as 12¼" or 12¾", use that measurement.

1. Cut strips 12½" wide with 6" x 24" ruler. Cut strips into squares with 12½" Square Up Ruler.

	12½" strip	into	**Squares**
Baby			1
Lap	1		2
Twin	3		8
Double	4		12
Queen	4		12
King	6		16

Corner Triangles

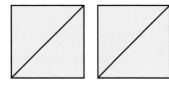

1. Cut two 9½" squares for every size quilt. If available, cut from leftovers of larger pieces.

2. Cut in half on one diagonal. Bias is on inside edge of sewn together quilt.

Sewing the Top Together

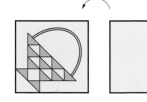

1. Lay out pieces on a large floor or table area, following charts on pages 165–166. Place so flowers of same color or shape are equally distributed throughout the quilt. Make number labels and pin to each block.

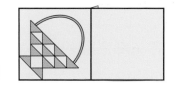

2. Sew one diagonal row together at a time in your planned order. Match and pin outside edges. Keep "crisp" points at Basket feet.

3. Press seams toward Solid Squares. Lay completed rows into position.

Sewing the Corner Triangles

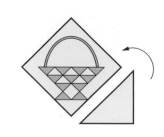

1. Flip Corner Triangles right sides together to Basket blocks. Center so that tips extend equally on both sides.

2. Pin the outside edges in place. Gently pat the triangle to fit the Basket block. Pin the center.

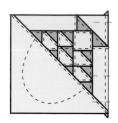

3. Sew all Corner Triangles with the triangle on the bottom. Do not allow the triangle to stretch. Be careful not to "cut off" the Basket Feet points with your stitching lines.

4. Gently press this seam toward the triangle from the wrong side.

5. Place the pieces back in the layout.

Sewing the Side Triangles to the Rows

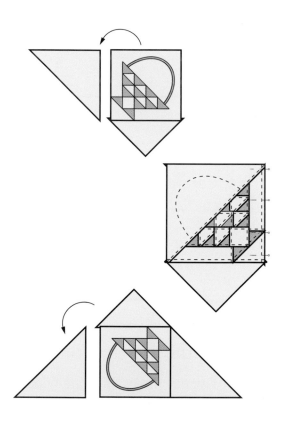

1. Flip the Basket block right sides together to the Side Triangle.

2. Pin, matching the square edge, and allowing a tip to hang over on the Corner Triangle. Gently pat the triangle to fit the Basket block.

3. Sew with the triangle on the bottom.

4. Press the seam toward the triangle. Outside edges must line up.

5. Place the sewn together row back in the layout.

6. Sew rows together.

7. Press top.

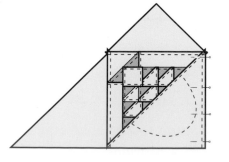

8. Straighten outside edges without removing ¼" seam allowance.

Place blocks so flowers of same color or shape are equally distributed throughout the quilt. Make number labels and pin to blocks.

Baby Quilt 4 Blocks

Lap Quilt 6 Blocks

King Quilt 25 Blocks

Extra Long Twin Quilt 15 Blocks
(May also be made with 12 Blocks)

Double and Queen Quilt 20 Blocks

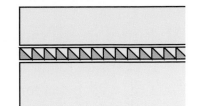

Making the Sawtooth Border

The Sawtooth Border consists of a 3½" Background strip, a strip of 2½" Pieced Squares, and a 5" Background strip.

	3½" strips	5" Strips
Baby	4	6
Lap	5	7
Twin	7	9
Double	9	10
Queen	9	10
King	10	11

Adding 3½" Strips

1. Straighten ends of 3½" Background strips.

2. Measure length of quilt down center and both sides. If measurements differ, take an average.

3. Sew strips together to make two strips longer than the length.

4. Cut strips to that measurement for both long sides.

5. Pin mid-point of strips to mid-point of quilt sides, both ends, and between every three inches.

6. Sew with a ¼" seam, stretching or easing as necessary. Repeat on opposite side.

7. Set seams, open, and press seams toward border.

8. Measure width of quilt across center, top, and bottom, including side borders. If the measurements differ, take an average.

9. Sew strips together for that measurement.

10. Pin to top and bottom, and sew.

11. Set seams, and press toward border.

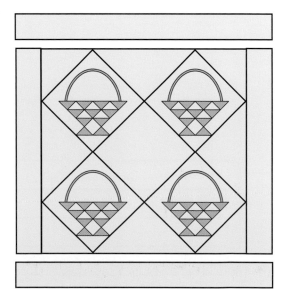

Baby Quilt with 3½" Border

167

Making Pieced Squares for Sawtooth Border

1. Cut Background and dark Basket fabrics into 9" strips. Cut 9" strips into 9" x 12" pieces for Pieced Squares.

	9" strips	into 9" x 12" pieces	Pieced Squares Needed
Baby	2	4	80
Lap	2	4	96
Twin	3	7	148
Double	3	7	166
Queen	3	7	166
King	3	8	184

2. Press Background and dark Basket 9" x 12" pieces right sides together. Draw a 3" grid and sew, following directions for Pieced Squares for Baskets on pages 32 to 34. Square pieces to 2½".

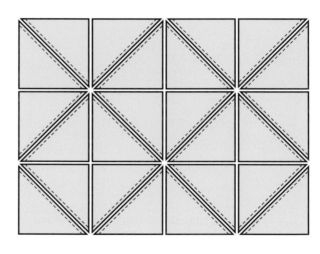

3. Count out four stacks, making a stack for each side.

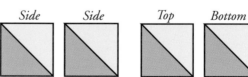

Place this many squares in each stack

	Two Sides	Top and Bottom
Baby	20 each	20 each
Lap	28 each	20 each
Twin	46 each	28 each
Double	46 each	37 each
Queen	46 each	37 each
King	46 each	46 each

Pieced Squares in Two Directions

1. Take stack for one side. Divide Pieced Squares into four equal stacks.

2. From these four, place two stacks with Pieced Squares turned in one direction, and two stacks with Pieced Squares turned in second direction.

3. Working with two stacks, flip right sides together and assembly-line sew. Press seams to one side.

4. Sew halves together. If your Pieced Squares are not exactly equal on each half, it will be hard to detect in a large finished quilt.

5. Match centers and measure sawtooth strip against side of quilt. You may need to remove one pieced square or take in some seams to make strip fit. Or you may sliver trim the 3½" border strip to fit sawtooth.

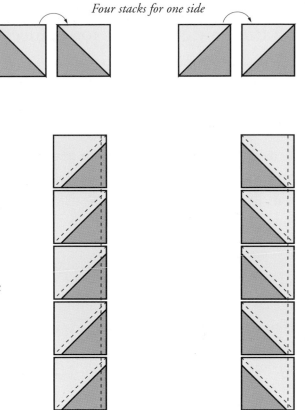

Four stacks for one side

6. Pin and sew sawtooth strip to sides.

7. Cut and sew 2½" Background squares to each end of top and bottom for corners.

8. Pin and sew to quilt top. Turn to page 181 for finishing.

Quilt with Lattice and Cornerstones

Cutting Striped Fabric for Lattice (Optional)

Striped fabric is cut with the grain lengthwise rather than selvage to selvage. The stripe you select should be approximately 3" wide plus a ¼" seam allowance on each side. Check the chart below for how many Lattice you need, and figure your yardage by the number of useable stripes. Cut Lattice the length of your block, plus ⅛" since lengthwise grain does not give.

For instance, there are twelve useable stripes in your stripe fabric. You need 48 lattice for your queen size quilt. Twelve divides into 48 four times. You need four selvage to selvage pieces the length of your block plus ⅛" or 50½". Round up to 54", or 1½" yards of striped fabric.

Anniversary Floral Style #247 Floral Vine, Color B

1. Unfold stripe fabric and place it on gridded cutting mat. Cut lengthwise on planned lines at planned width one layer at a time, using 6" x 24" ruler.

2. Cut Lattice the measurement of your Basket block, plus ⅛".

3. Cut Cornerstones into squares the same width as the lattice. See chart below.

Quilt	Lattice
Baby	16
Lap	24
Twin	32
Double	48
Queen	48
King	64

Cutting Lattice from Fabric other than Stripe

1. Cut 3½" strips selvage to selvage. Trim off selvages.

2. Cut each Lattice the measurement of your Basket block. You should get three Lattice from each strip.

3. Cut 3½" square Cornerstones.

	Strips	Lattice	Strips	Cornerstones
Baby	6	16	1	12
Lap	8	24	2	17
Twin	11	32	2	22
Double	16	48	3	31
Queen	16	48	3	31
King	22	64	4	40

Planning Your Block Placement

1. Lay out blocks on floor area.

2. Place blocks so flowers of same color or shape are equally distributed throughout quilt.

3. Make number labels and pin to each block.

4. Stack the blocks in order as numbered, keeping Number 1 on top.

Baby Quilt 5 Blocks

King Quilt 25 Blocks

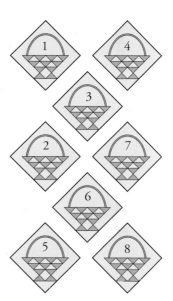

Lap Quilt 8 Blocks

Twin Quilt 11 Blocks

Double or Queen Quilt 18 Blocks

Sewing Lattice to Basket Blocks

1. Place stacked blocks in this order with Number 1 on top.

2. Make two stacks of Lattice and one stack of Cornerstones equal to the number of Basket blocks. Set the remaining pieces aside.

3. Flip Lattice right sides together to Basket block. Sew. Flip Cornerstone right sides together to Lattice. Match outside edges, and sew.

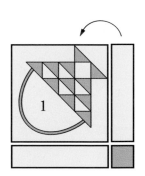

4. Assembly-line sew all pieces together.

5. Clip threads after every Cornerstone.

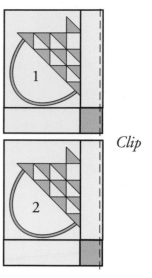

Clip

6. Restack in numbered order with Number 1 on top.

7. Flip Cornerstone and Lattice right sides together to Basket block. Match seam, pushing seam underneath toward Lattice and seam on top toward Lattice. Assembly-line sew.

8. Clip apart threads holding the blocks together according to the number of Basket blocks in each diagonal row. See charts on pages 179–180.

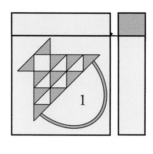

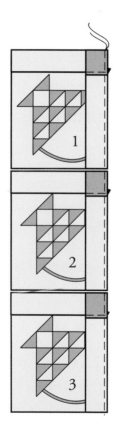

Baby	Clip after Block 1 and Block 4
Lap	Clip after Block 1, Block 4, and Block 7
Twin	Clip after Block 1, Block 4, Block 7, and Block 10
Double	Clip after Block 1, Block 4, Block 9, Block 14 and Block 17
Queen	Clip after Block 1, Block 4, Block 9, Block 14, and Block 17
King	Clip after Block 1, Block 4, Block 9, Block 16, Block 21, and Block 24

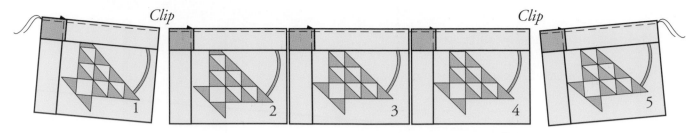

Example of a Baby Quilt - Clip apart after Block 1 and Block 4

9. Sew chained together blocks into single diagonal rows. Fingerpress both seams up at Cornerstones.

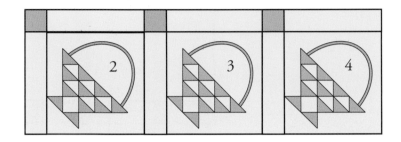

Sewing Remaining Lattice and Cornerstones

1. Stack the pieces, and assembly-line sew.

2. Sew last Cornerstone to opposite end of last Lattice. Set aside for single Basket block in bottom right corner of quilt.

3. Press seam toward Lattice. Clip threads.

4. Sew single Lattice/Cornerstone to right end of each diagonal row as indicated by highlighted areas.

5. Sew Lattice with two Cornerstones to bottom right corner block.

6. Press seams toward Lattice.

7. Lay out diagonal rows in order.

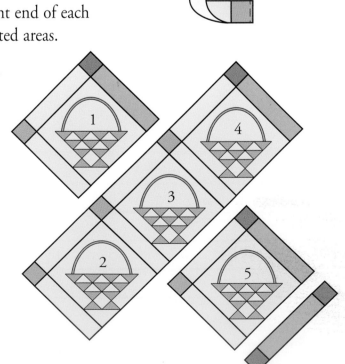

Cutting Side Triangles

1. Cut this many 22¼" squares for Side Triangles:

Baby	1
Lap	2
Twin	2
Double	3
Queen	3
King	3

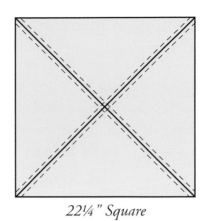

22¼ " Square

2. Line up yardstick or two rulers on diagonal and draw a line. Line up on second diagonal, and draw a second line. Stay stitch on both sides of diagonal line.

3. Cut on both diagonals. Do not move the square until after the second cut.

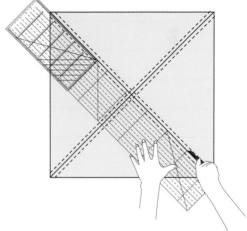

4. Place a Side Triangle at left end of each row and across top of quilt. Smaller triangles will be placed at corners.

5. Flip each Triangle right sides together to its row. Match the square bottom, and let the tip of the Triangle hang over at top. Pin outside edges. Gently pat Triangle to fit. Pin center.

6. Sew with Triangle on bottom. Place each row back in layout.

Across top

Left end

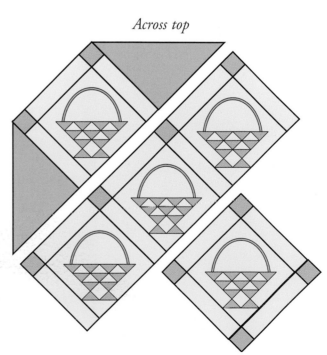

Completing Triangles for Bottom Edge

1. Stack appropriate number of Lattice/Cornerstones and Triangles.

2. Flip Lattice right sides together to Triangle. Match square bottom, and let tip of Triangle extend at top. Pin and sew with Triangle on bottom. Ease in Triangle if necessary.

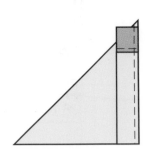

3. Press seams away from Triangle.

4. Place in empty spaces across bottom of quilt.

Baby	1
Lap	1
Twin	1
Double	2
Queen	2
King	3

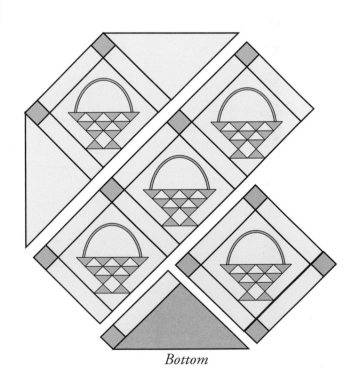

Bottom

Completing Triangles for Right Side of Quilt

1. Stack appropriate number of Lattice/Cornerstones and Triangles.

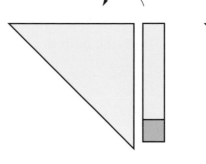
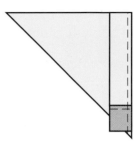

Baby	1
Lap	2
Twin	3
Double	3
Queen	3
King	3

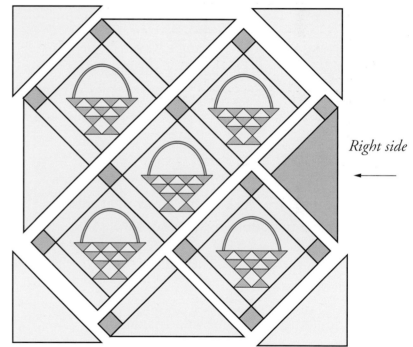

2. Flip Lattice right sides together to Triangle. Match square top, and let tip of Triangle extend at bottom. Pin and sew with Triangle on bottom. Ease in Triangle if necessary.

3. Press seams away from Triangle.

4. Place in empty spaces across right side of quilt.

Right side

Cutting Corner Triangles

1. Cut two 14" squares in half on one diagonal.

2. Place at four corners of quilt.

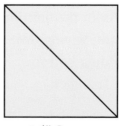
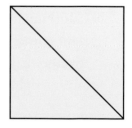

14" Square

Sewing Rows of Quilt Top Together

Examine your quilt rows closely and compare to your layout diagram. Make certain that all pieces are in proper placement. To avoid mistakes, the safest and easiest way to sew the quilt together is to lay the rows back in position each time before another piece is added.

The quilt is sewn together from the bottom right corner upward.

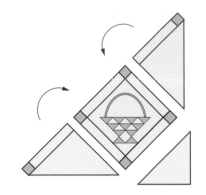

Sewing the Bottom Right Corner

1. Flip Side Triangles right sides together to block. Match and pin square edges. Let tip hang over at the bottom. Sew with triangle on bottom.

2. Fold out and flat. Press seams away from Side Triangle.

3. Pin and sew Corner Triangle with triangle on bottom, and tips hanging out equally on each end.

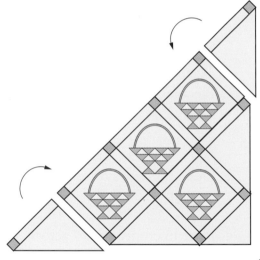

Sewing Next Diagonal Row to Corner

1. Flip the three block diagonal row right sides together to bottom right corner row.

2. Match, pin and sew. The outside edges must line up.

3. Add bottom and right Side Triangles.

Finishing the Top

1. Continue to sew from the bottom right corner upward, sewing rows together before adding bottom and/or right Side Triangles.

2. Sew on remaining Corner Triangles.

3. Press seams toward Lattice.

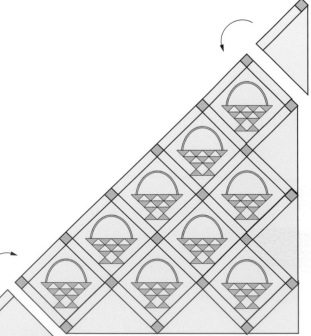

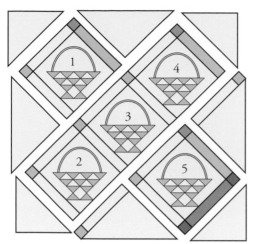

Baby Quilt 5 Blocks

Lap Quilt 8 Blocks

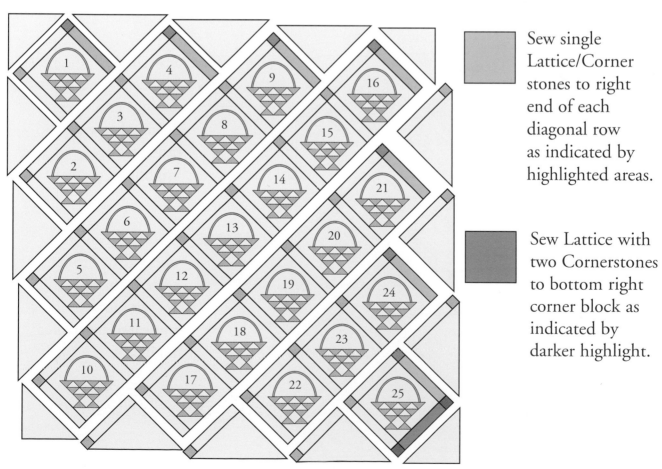

King Quilt 25 Blocks

Sew single Lattice/Corner stones to right end of each diagonal row as indicated by highlighted areas.

Sew Lattice with two Cornerstones to bottom right corner block as indicated by darker highlight.

Extra Long Twin Quilt 11 Blocks
(You may want to make a Lap for twin bed.)

Sew single Lattice/Cornerstones to right end of each diagonal row as indicated by highlighted areas.

Sew Lattice with two Cornerstones to bottom right corner block as indicated by darker highlight.

Double or Queen Quilt 18 Blocks

Finishing

Check the Fit

Lay the quilt top on your bed before adding the last borders and backing. Measure to find how much border you need to get the fit you want. Keep in mind, the quilt will "shrink" approximately 2" in length and width after completion of machine quilting.

Adding Borders

1. Square off the selvage edges, and sew strips together lengthwise.

2. Measure the long sides of the quilt.

3. Cut two pieces the same length from the border fabric.

4. Pin the borders to the long sides.

5. Stitch from end to end. Fold them out flat.

6. Measure the top and bottom of the quilt from one outside edge to the other, including the borders just added.

7. Cut two borders that measurement.

8. Pin the borders to the top and bottom.

9. Stitch. Fold them out flat.

Marking Your Quilt

Select a continuous line feather stencil to fit in the Solid Square blocks. Half of the same stencil can be used in the Side Triangles, and one fourth in the Corner Triangles. Feathers are free-motion machine quilted.

Select a continuous line cable stencil to fit in the outside border for free motion machine quilting or quilting with a walking foot. Select a marking pencil that will show on your background fabric, as a silver pencil or disappearing pen.

1. Press your quilt top from the wrong side, and then the right side.

2. Center the feather stencil on each Solid Square. Lightly trace in the lines so you can see them without straining your eyes. Trace part of the stencil on the Side and Corner Triangles.

3. On the border stencil, draw a 45° line across the corner for accurate placement on the quilt top. Measure the cable pattern from end of corner to where pattern begins repeat again. See dots.

4. Mark the four corner cables first.

5. Measure side of quilt from end of one corner cable to beginning of opposite corner cable.

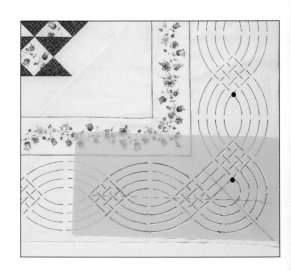

6. Divide the repeat measurement into quilt measurement for the number of cables to draw on that side. The repeat may not divide into side evenly. If so, the size of each cable can be adjusted by making it slightly elongated or slighter shorter so repeat cables fit equally. If the remainder is close to the length of the repeat, then shorten each cable slightly. If the remainder is a few inches, elongate each cable equally.

7. Mark the outside cable first, and shorten or lengthen according to your calculations by sliding the stencil. Mark the inside lines.

Layering the Quilt

1. Spread out the backing on a large table or floor area with the right side down. Clamp the fabric to the edge of the table with quilt clips or tape the backing to the floor. Do not stretch the backing.

2. Layer the batting on top of the backing, and pat flat.

3. With the quilt top right side up, center on the backing. Smooth until all layers are flat. Clamp or tape outside edges.

4. Safety pin the layers together every three to five inches. Use a pinning tool to assist the process. Pin next to your machine quilting lines.

Machine Quilting Your Top

The ideal machine quilting area is a sewing machine bed level with the table, and a large area to the left of the machine to support the quilt. Machine quilt on a day when you are relaxed to help avoid muscle strain down your neck, shoulders, and back. Sit in a raised stenographer's chair so your arms can rest on the table.

"Stitch in the Ditch" to Anchor the Blocks and Borders

1. Thread your machine with matching thread or invisible thread. If you use invisible thread, loosen your top tension. Match the bobbin thread to the backing.

2. Attach your walking foot, and lengthen the stitch to 8 to 10 stitches per inch or 3.5 on computerized machines.

3. Roll on the diagonal to the center. Clip the rolls in place.

4. Spread the seams open, and "stitch in the ditch."

5. Unroll the quilt to the next diagonal seam. Clip the roll in place, and "stitch in the ditch."

6. Continue to unroll and roll the quilt until all the seams are stitched, anchoring the blocks.

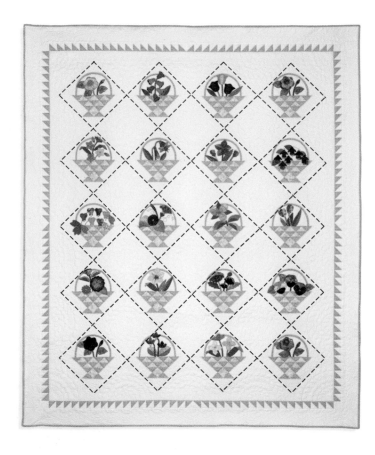

Free Motion Machine Quilting

The easiest way to quilt the blocks is by free motion machine quilting around each flower piece and Basket Handle either "in the ditch" or ¼" away. If you are a novice at this technique, imperfections are easily hidden by using invisible thread and "stitching in the ditch." Use a darning foot and drop or cover feed dogs with a plate. No stitch length is required as you control the length. Use a fine needle and a little hole throat plate with a center needle position. Use invisible or regular thread in the top and regular thread to match the backing in the bobbin. Loosen the top tension if using invisible thread.

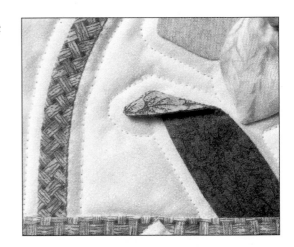

1. Bring the bobbin thread up on the edge of the applique, or ¼" away. Lower the needle into the background fabric and drop the foot. Moving the fabric very slowly, take a few tiny stitches to lock them. Snip off the tails of the threads.

2. With your eyes watching the outline of the block ahead of the needle, and your fingertips stretching the fabric and acting as a quilting hoop, move the fabric in a steady motion while the machine is running at a constant speed. By moving the fabric underneath the needle side to side, and forward and backward, outline the Handle and the flowers. Lock off the tiny stitches and clip the threads at the end.

3. "Stitch in the ditch" in the seams on your Basket with either the darning foot or the walking foot.

4. Use this same free motion technique to machine quilt fabric patterns in Solid Squares, Side and Corner Triangles.

Free Motion Stippling

Free motion stippling is an over-
all meandering design. Because it
is "free form," marking is not
necessary. The machine set up
and technique are the same as
free motion quilting, but the
background is "filled" with
meandering stitches.

Quilted by Carol Selepec

Set up a practice swatch of the three layers
to become comfortable with moving the
fabric to make your desired size stitch.
Adjust the tension for either invisible or regular thread. Practice moving your hands
back and forward and sideways, but not
turning the swatch. The quilt at the top was
quilted on a professional quilting machine.

*Quilted by
Teresa Varnes*

Adding the Binding

Use a walking foot attachment and
regular thread on top and in the bobbin
to match the binding.

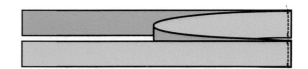

1. Square off the selvage edges, and
   sew 3" strips together lengthwise.

2. Fold and press in half with wrong
   sides together.

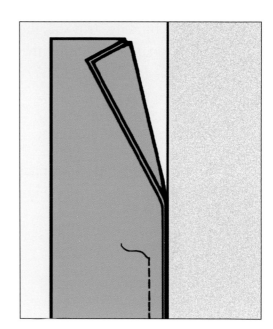

3. Line up the raw edges of the folded
   binding with the raw edges of the
   quilt in the middle of one side.

4. Begin stitching 4" from the end
   of the binding.

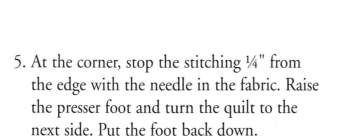

5. At the corner, stop the stitching ¼" from
   the edge with the needle in the fabric. Raise
   the presser foot and turn the quilt to the
   next side. Put the foot back down.

6. Stitch backwards ¼" to the edge of the
   binding, raise the foot, and pull the quilt
   forward slightly.

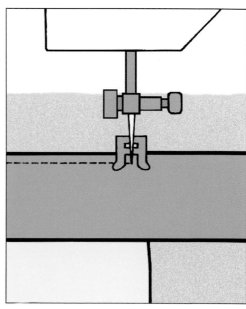

7. Fold the binding strip straight up on the diagonal. Fingerpress the diagonal fold.

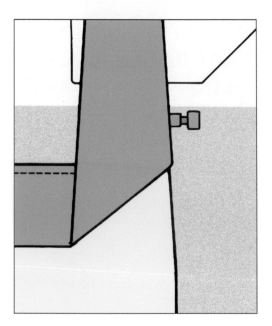

8. Fold the binding strip straight down with the diagonal fold underneath. Line up the top of the fold with the raw edge of the binding underneath.

9. Begin sewing from the edge.

10. Continue stitching and mitering the corners around the outside of the quilt.

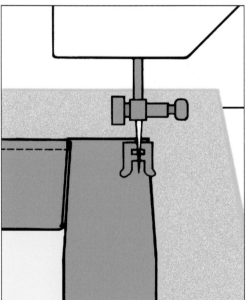

11. Stop stitching 4" from where the ends will overlap.

12. Line up the two ends of binding. Trim the excess with a ½" overlap.

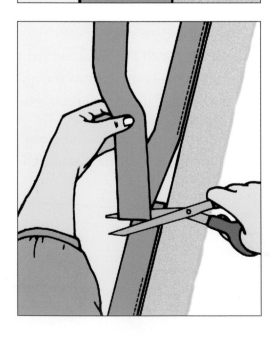

13. Open out the folded ends and pin right sides together. Sew a ¼" seam.

14. Continue to stitch the binding in place.

15. Trim the batting and backing up to the raw edges of the binding.

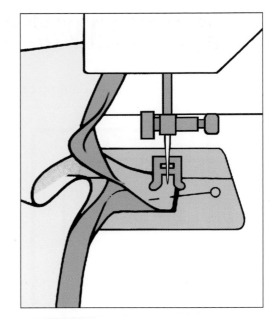

16. Fold the binding to the back side of the quilt. Pin in place so that the folded edge on the binding covers the stitching line. Tuck in the excess fabric at each miter on the diagonal.

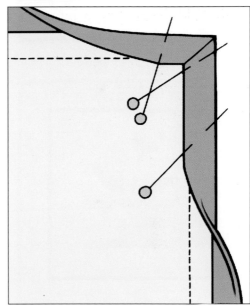

17. From the right side, "stitch in the ditch" using invisible thread on the front side, and a bobbin thread to match the binding on the back side. Catch the folded edge of the binding on the back side with the stitching.

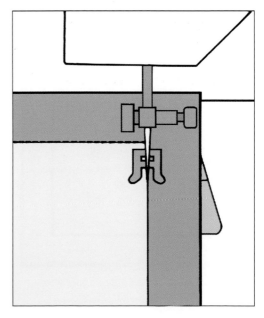

One Block Wallhanging   Finished Size: 24" Square

Make either the traditional pieced Basket or the Easy Basket.

Poppy Block *Instructions on page 84.*

Jonquil Block *Instructions on page 132.*

Bluet Block *Instructions on page 138.*

Pansy Block *Instructions on page 90.*

Zinnia Block *Instructions on page 156.*

Jonquil Block *Instructions on page 132.*

Yardage

One Flower

Select the flower of your choice. Yardages for the flowers are found on pages 58–161.

Pieced Basket   or   Easy Basket

Background
    ½ yd
        Top
            (1) 13¼" square
        Sides
            (2) 2¾" x 10" pieces
        Bottom
            (1) 5½" square

Medium
    ⅛ yd
        Pieced Squares
            (1) 3" x 9"
        Bottom Square
            (1) 2½" square

Dark
    ⅜ yd
        Handle
            (1) 1⅜" x 18" bias strip
        Top Edge
            (1) 4½" square
        Pieced Squares
            (1) 3" x 9" piece
        Feet
            (1) 3" square

Background
    ½ yd
        Top
            (1) 13¼" square
        Sides
            (2) 2¾" x 10" strips
        Bottom
            (1) 5½" square

Medium
    ¼ yd
        Basket
            (1) 7"
        Bottom
            (1) 2½" square

Dark
    ⅜ yd
        Handle
            (1) 1⅜" x 18" bias strip
        Basket
            (2) 2½" x 8" pieces
        Feet
            (1) 3" square

Finishing

Corner Triangles
    ⅓ yd
        (2) 10½" squares

Floral Border
    ½ yd
        (4) 3½" strips
or

Striped Border
    ¾ yd
        (4) 3½" x 27" strips

Folded Border
    ⅛ yd
        (2) 1¼" strips

Binding
    ⅓ yd
        (3) 3" strips

Batting and Backing
    28" square

Finishing Your One Block Wallhanging

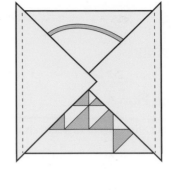

1. Make one Basket block. Pieced Basket instructions are on pages 28–43. Easy Basket instructions are on pages 195–197.

2. Sew selected flower to Handle piece. Sew Basket together and square to 12½".

3. Cut 10½" squares in half on one diagonal, making four Corner Triangles.

4. Center and pin two triangles on two opposite sides of block. Measure tips so that they extend equally on both sides, approximately 1".

5. Stitch in place. Press triangles out, and add two remaining triangles.

6. Place on gridded cutting board, lining up two sides with grid. Sliver trim to straighten edge. **Allow ⅝" seam allowance to accommodate folded border.**

7. **Folded Border:** Cut 1¼" strips in half. With wrong sides together, press strips in half lengthwise.

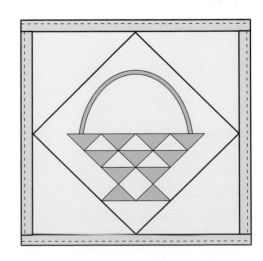

8. **Lengthen stitch to 10 stitches per inch, or setting #3.** Sew strips to two opposite sides of wallhanging with seam slightly less than ¼". Do not press out. Add two remaining Folded Borders, overlapping in corners.

Adding Border Stripe with Mitered Corner

Stripe: Allow ¼" seam allowance on each side of stripes.

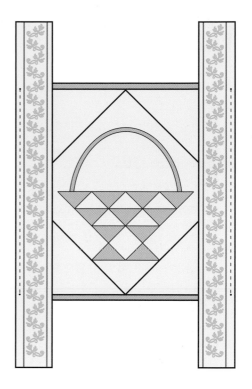

1. Center and pin borders on two opposite sides of wallhanging. Border should extend at least 4" at each end. Along seam allowance, mark a dot at each end, ¼" in from edge. Sew between the marked dots, and backstitch at each end. Press away from folded border.

2. Add two remaining borders, meeting in corners ¼" from edge.

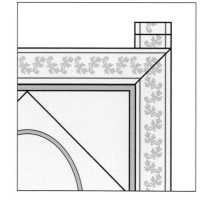

3. To miter, place corner on ironing board. Fold top strip under diagonally, and line up the two border strips. Press diagonal crease with iron.
   Place Square Up ruler's 45° line on seam. Check that corner is square.

4. **Finishing Option One:** Pin in place. Sew from right side with blind hem stitch and invisible thread, straight stitch, or hand stitch.

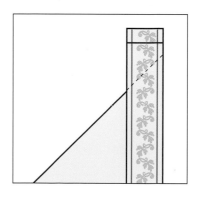

5. **Finishing Option Two:** Open wrong side up. Pin through the lines at the crease, lining up the two strips. Sew along the diagonal crease starting at ¼" dot. Trim seam allowance and press open.

6. Machine quilt and bind.

Four Easy Baskets Wallhanging

Eleanor Burns Approximate Finished Size: 36" square

Yardage

Tulips – page 150

> ¼ yd light to medium weight non-woven fusible interfacing
>
> ⅛ yd each of three tulip colors
>
> ⅛ yd each of two greens
>
> Matching thread

Baskets

Background
½ yd

> (1) 13¼" strip for Top
> > (2) 13¼" squares
>
> (2) 2¾" strips for Sides
> > (8) 2¾" x 10" strips
>
> (2) 5½" squares for Bottom

Medium
¼ yd

> (1) 7" square for Basket
>
> (4) 2½" squares for Bottom

Dark
½ yd

> (1) 13½" strip for Handles
> > (4) 1⅜" x 18" bias strips
>
> (2) 2½" strips for Basket
> > (8) 2½" x 8" pieces
>
> (4) 3" squares for Feet

Finishing

Corner Triangles
⅓ yd
> > (2) 10" squares

Floral Border
⅔ yd
> > (4) 5½" strips

or Striped Border with Eight Repeats
⅔ yd
> (8) 5¼"–5½" x 24" stripes

Striped Border with Four Repeats
1¼ yds
> > (4) 5¼"–5½" x 45" stripes

Folded Border
¼ yd
(Optional)
> > (4) 1¼" strips

Binding
⅜ yd
> > (4) 3" strips

Batting
40" x 40"

Backing
1¼ yds

Making Handle Pieces

1. **Top:** Draw diagonal line on 13¼" Background square. Staystitch on both sides of diagonal line. Press. Cut on diagonal line. Crease in half.

2. Trace Handle pattern on Top. Page 28.

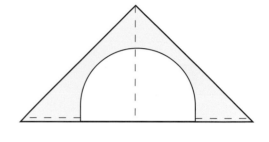

3. **Handle:** Press 1⅜" x 18" bias strip in half wrong sides together.

4. Line up raw edges of bias with Handle line. **Stretch bias slightly** as you sew with ¼" seam around curve.

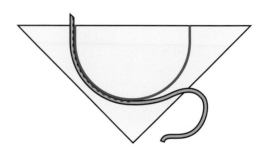

5. Fold over and press with steam.

6. Sew folded edge of bias strip with blind hem stitch by hand or machine.

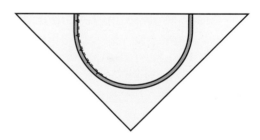

Making Basket Blocks

1. **Baskets:** Cut 7" medium square into fourths on both diagonals. Stack right side up.

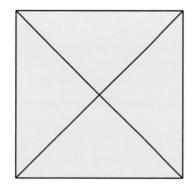

2. Place medium Triangle in this order with 2½" medium square and two dark 2½" x 8" strips.

3. Flip second row right sides together to first row. Assembly-line sew.

4. Press seams toward dark.

5. Sew second seam. Press toward medium triangle.

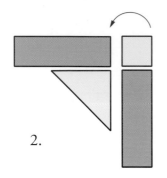

2.

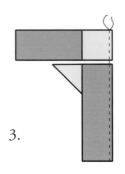

3.

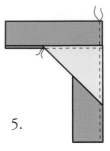

5.

6. **Feet:** Cut 3" dark square in half on one diagonal.

7. Sew Feet to 2¾" x 10" Background Sides. Press seams toward dark.

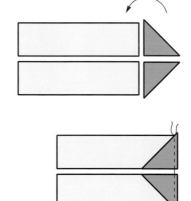

8. Match seam and sew first Side to Basket. Press seam toward Background.

9. Match seam and sew second Side to Basket. Press seam toward Background.

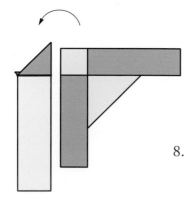

8.

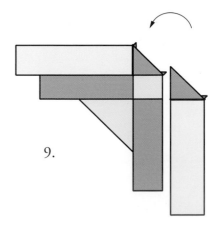

9.

10. **Bottom:** Cut 5½" Background square in half on one diagonal.

11. Straighten Basket's bottom edge, maintaining ¼" seam allowance. Center triangle right sides together on Basket, and sew. Press seam toward Bottom.

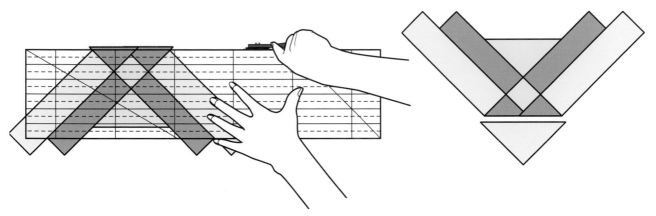

12. Using 6" x 24" ruler, place ruler's 5¾" line on Bottom seam, and trim top of Basket so Basket is 5¾" wide.

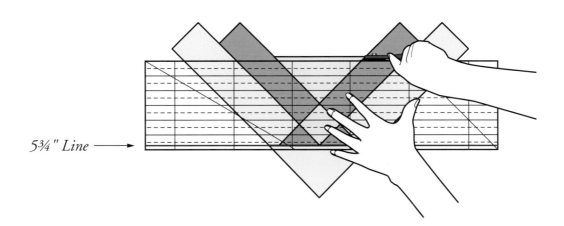

5¾" Line ⟶

13. Make tulips and sew to Handle piece. *Pages 150–155.*

14. **Handle Top:** Pin and sew to Basket. Press seam toward Basket.

15. Square to 12½", maintaining ¼" seams at Feet.

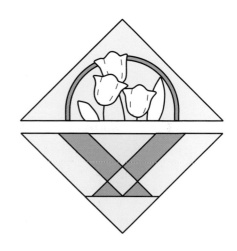

197

Finishing the Four Block Basket Quilt

1. Sew four blocks together. Press seams in opposite directions.

2. **Optional Folded Border:** Press 1¼" strips in half lengthwise wrong sides together.

3. Lay folded strip on right side of 5½" Border strip, matching raw edges. Sew ⅛" from raw edges with 10 stitches per inch or #3 setting.

4. **Corner Triangles:** Draw diagonal line on two 10" squares.

5. Staystitch ⅛" from both sides of diagonal line.

6. Cut two 10" squares in half on one diagonal.

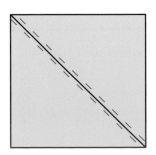

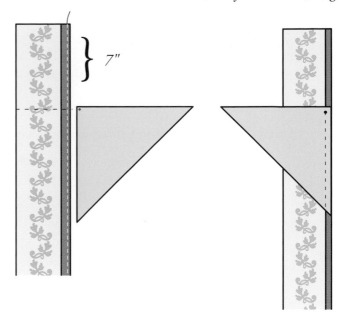

7. Lay out Border and Corner Triangle. Measure down 7" from end of Border.

8. Flip Triangle to Border and start sewing ¼" from edge of Triangle in order to miter Borders. See dot on Triangle.

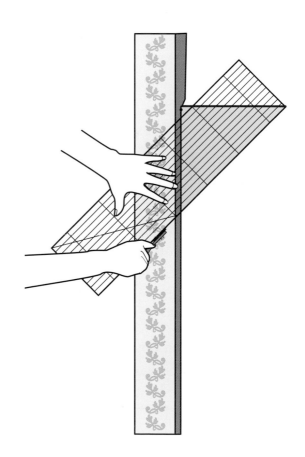

9. Open and press seam away from Triangle. Press Folded Border toward Border. Lay 6" x 24" ruler along long edge of Triangle, lining up 45º line. Trim off excess.

10. Use Border excess or new strip for other side of Triangle. Measure 7" from end of Border. Pin and sew toward corner, leaving ¼" of Triangle free where Borders meet.

11. Open and press seam toward Triangle. Press Folded Border toward Border.

12. Place ruler across edge of Triangle with 45° line on Border's edge. Trim off excess.

13. Repeat with remaining three Triangle corners.

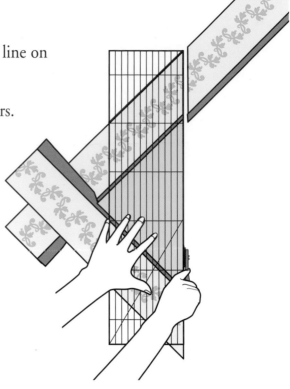

Mitering Corners

To miter, place corner on ironing board. Fold top strip under diagonally, and line up the two border stripes. Press diagonal crease with iron. Place ruler's 45° line on seam. Check that corner is square.

Finishing Option One: Pin in place. Sew from right side with blind hem stitch and invisible thread, straight stitch, or hand stitch. Repeat with remaining Corners. Trim seams to ¼" and press open.

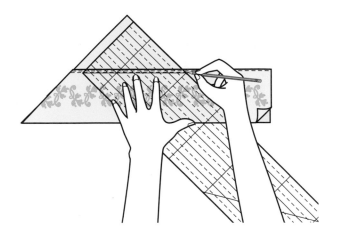

Finishing Option Two: Open wrong side up. Draw a diagonal line on crease. Pin through the lines at the crease, lining up the two strips. Sew along the diagonal crease starting at ¼" dot. Trim seam allowance and press open. Repeat with remaining Corners. Trim seams to ¼" and press open.

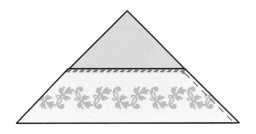

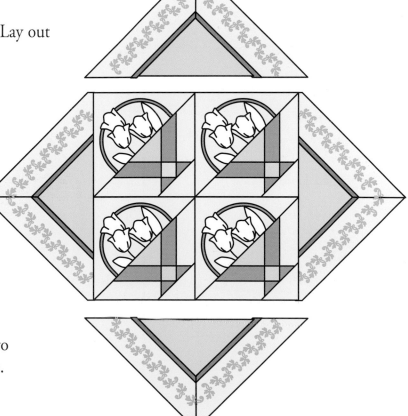

1. **Sewing Triangles to Border:** Lay out Triangles next to quilt top.

2. Finger crease center of each Triangle and match with seams of quilt.

3. Pin bias edge to quilt on opposite corners. Sew carefully so bias does not stretch. Fold out. Press seams toward Border. Square off excess with top.

4. Pin and sew on remaining two sides, matching outside edges.

5. Machine quilt and bind.

Small Basket Wallhanging

Yardage

Baskets

Background
½ yd
(2) 4" strips
into (13) 4" squares
(2) 2¼" strips
into (13) 2¼" x 4¼" rectangles

Baskets and Feet – Medium and Dark
(13) assorted 4" squares

Handles
2 yds Clover ¼" Quick Fusible Bias Tape

Eleanor Burns   Approximate Finished Size: 26" Square
Basket Finished Size: 4½" Square

Finishing

Side and Corner Triangles
¼ yd
(2) 7¾" squares
(2) 4¼" squares

Folded Border
⅛ yd
(2) 1¼" strips

Floral Border
⅓ yd
(3) 3½" strips

or Striped Border
⅞ yd
(4) 3½" strips

Binding
⅓ yd
(3) 3" strips

Backing and Batting
(1) 30" square of each

Trace on 4" square template plastic.

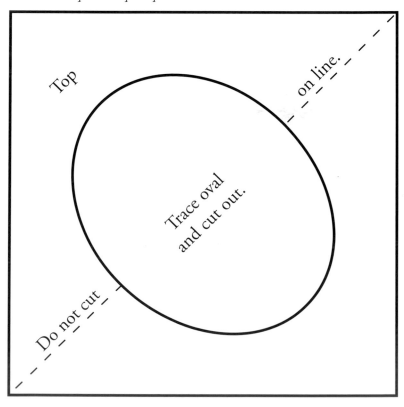

Making the Handle Piece

Each 4" Background Square makes two handle pieces.

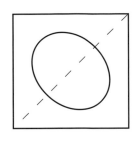

1. Trace template on 4" square template plastic.
   Cut out oval.

2. Count out seven 4" Background squares. Cut one in
   half on diagonal.

3. Carefully center template on right side of six squares.
   Draw around oval. Trace half oval on half square.

4. Cut six squares in half on one diagonal, following
   dashed line.

5. **Clover ¼" Fusible Bias Tape:** Cut bias tape into
   thirteen 5" pieces.

6. Line up left side of bias with line on right.

7. Press bias in place around curve. Use a steam iron.

*So you don't burn your fingers, hold last inch of bias tape
with stiletto and press in place.*

8. From wrong side, trim ends of bias tape.

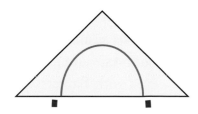

Making the Basket and Feet

1. Stack several 4" Basket squares at a time. With a 6" square ruler, cut in half on one diagonal. Stack left half for Basket.

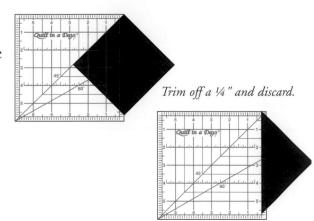

Trim off a ¼" and discard.

2. Line up ruler's ¼" line on right half, and trim off ¼". Stack for Feet in same fabric order as Basket.

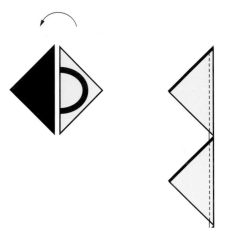

3. Place Basket next to Handle. Flip right sides together. Match outside edges of Basket and Handle. Assembly-line sew.

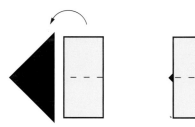

4. **Press 2¼" x 4¼" Background strips** in half widthwise. Place Feet next to Background strips. Center strip on Feet. Line up fold with tip. Assembly-line sew.

5. Press with Basket and Feet wrong side up, and set seams. Open and press seams. Do not press out crease. Clip threads. Trim tips even with Basket.

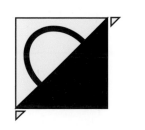

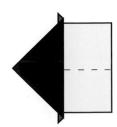

6. Cut Feet in half, lining up ruler with fold in strip. *It's not important that the cut be in the exact center of the triangle.* As you cut, make two stacks.

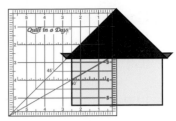

Cut strip at 2⅛".

7. Line up Feet with Basket, **allowing an extra ⅛" at top.** Flip right sides together. Assembly-line sew.

8. Press with Feet wrong side up, and set seam. Open and press. From wrong side, clip off tips even with Basket, and stack.

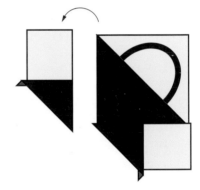

9. Line up Feet with Basket, **allowing an extra ⅛" at top.** Flip right sides together, and assembly-line sew.

10. Press with Feet wrong side up, and set seam. Open and press seam toward Feet.

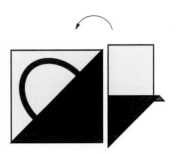

Squaring up the Block

1. Place ruler's 45° line on Foot seam, and ¼" line on Basket's bottom seam. Manipulate ruler so straight edge touches outside points. Trim.

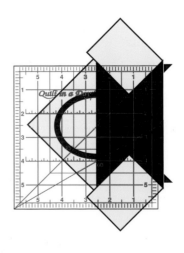

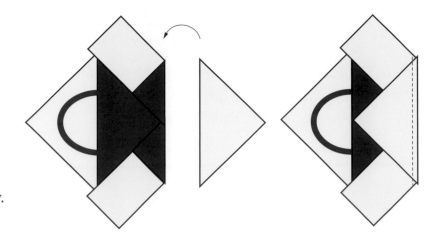

2. Cut six remaining 4"
   Background squares in
   half for Bottoms.

3. Flip Bottom right sides
   together to Basket and
   center. Assembly-line sew.

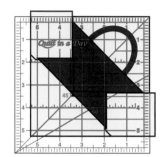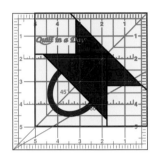

4. Press with Bottom wrong side
   up, and set seam. Open and
   press seam toward Bottom.

5. Square to 5". *Depending on your
   seam allowance, you may need to
   square your blocks to another
   consistent size, as 5⅛" or 4¾", so
   you don't trim off seam allowance.*

Sewing the Top Together

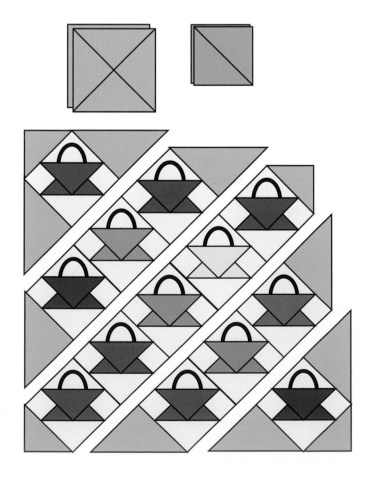

1. Lay out blocks.

2. Cut the two 7¾" squares in
   fourths on both diagonals.
   Place around sides.

3. Cut the two 4¼" squares in
   half on one diagonal. Place
   in corners.

4. Sew rows together. Match
   square edges and allow ⅜"
   tips at opposite ends,
   carefully easing in triangles.

5. Sew top together. Press seams
   away from center.

6. Add border, machine quilt,
   and bind.

Salvage Sally Wallhanging

Eleanor Burns   *Approximate Finished Size: 33" Square*

Yardage

Blocks

Baskets
(5) different 4½" x 7" rectangles

Flowers
(5) different 4" squares

Leaves
⅛ yd

Background
⅔ yd
    (1) 8" strip into
        (5) 8" squares for blocks
    (1) 14" square for side triangles
    (2) 8¼" squares for corners

Light to Medium Weight Non-woven Fusible Interfacing
½ yd

Finishing

Lattice and Binding
⅔ yd
    (4) 2" strips into
        (16) 2" x 8" strips for Lattice
    (4) 3" strips for Binding

Cornerstones and Folded Border
¼ yd
    (12) 2" squares for Cornerstones
    (4) 1¼" strips for Folded Border

Border
½ yd
    (4) 3½" strips

Backing and Batting
1 yd

Additional Supplies
Template plastic
10 assorted buttons

Be a thrifty "Salvage Sally" and rescue gay bits of fabric from your scrap-bag to make these flower basket appliques for a quilt. Use a different print for each flower, plain material for the baskets. An inexpensive way to brighten a bedroom!

207

Making the Blocks

1. Trace patterns on template plastic and cut out.

2. Trace five Baskets and five Flowers on interfacing, including the dotted line.

3. Trace eight Leaves on interfacing end to end with ¼" space between each for easy sewing.

4. Cut the Baskets and Flowers apart. Leave the Leaves in long strip.

5. Place traced Baskets and Flowers with dotted, fusible side of interfacing on right side of appropriate fabric. Sew on lines with 20 stitches per inch. Sew Leaves with continuous stitching.

6. Trim. Cut Flowers and Leaves in half on dotted lines. Clip a small hole in interfacing on wider part of Basket. Turn right side out and press with a wooden iron.

7. Cut cotton batting same size as Baskets and Flowers. Stuff using hemostats.

8. Center pieces on 8" Background square and fuse in place.

9. Stitch around outside edges with blanket stitch and colored thread, **or** blind hem stitch and invisible thread.

10. Sew buttons to centers of flowers.

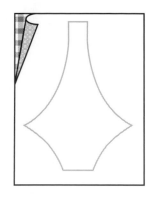

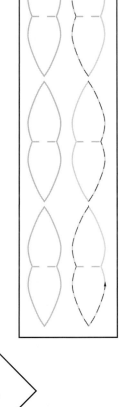
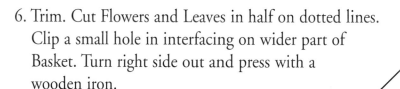
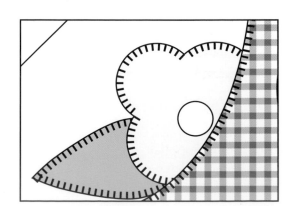

Sewing Diagonal Rows Together

1. Lay out blocks and plan placement. Pin number labels to blocks. Stack in order with one on top.

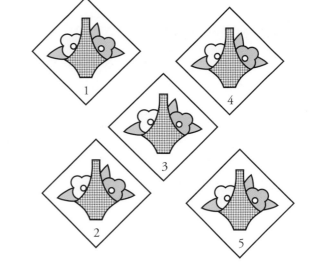

2. Place Baskets with five Cornerstones and two stacks of five Lattice.

3. Flip the top Lattice right sides together to the Cornerstone. Sew. Flip the Block right sides together to the Lattice. Match outside edges, and assembly-line sew.

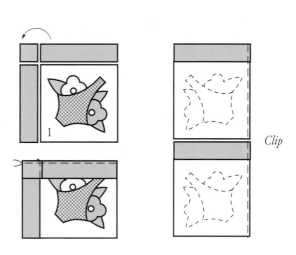

Clip

4. Clip the threads **after every Block.**

5. Open flat and stack right side up.

6. Flip the Cornerstones and Lattice right sides together to the block. **Push seam underneath toward the Lattice and the seam on top toward the Lattice,** and assembly-line sew all pieces.

7. Clip the threads holding the blocks together **after the first and fourth blocks.**

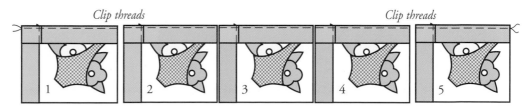

Clip threads   *Clip threads*

8. Sew remaining seams in middle row, **pressing both seams up at Cornerstones.**

9. Lay out diagonal rows.

Sewing Remaining Lattice and Cornerstones

1. Stack remaining Lattice and Cornerstones and assembly-line sew.

2. Sew last Cornerstone to opposite end of last Lattice.

3. **Press seams toward Lattice.** Clip connecting threads.

4. Sew a Lattice/Cornerstone to the right end of each diagonal row.

5. Sew Cornerstone/Lattice/Cornerstone to the bottom right corner block.

6. **Press seams toward Lattice.**

7. Cut 14" Background square on both diagonals.

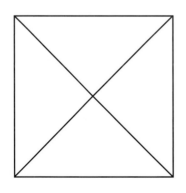

8. Sew one Lattice/Cornerstone to one triangle cut from 14" Background square.

9. Sew last Lattice/Cornerstone to second triangle.

10. **Press seams toward Lattice.**

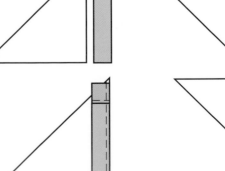

Sewing Top Together

1. Lay out rows of blocks with Side Triangles.

2. Flip each Side Triangle right sides together to its row. Match square edges, and let a ⅜" tip on Triangle hang over on opposite end. Pin outside edges. Gently pat Triangle to fit. Pin center.

3. Sew with Triangle on the bottom.

4. **Press seams away from Triangles.**

5. Sew rows together, lining up the outside edges.

6. **Press seams toward Lattice.**

7. Cut two 8¼" squares in half on one diagonal for Corner Triangles.

8. Sew to quilt top last.

Finishing the Wallhanging

1. Lay pressed top on a gridded cutting mat, and check if sides need to be straightened.

2. Sliver trim the Side and Corner Triangles, allowing a little more than ¼" for Folded Border.

3. **Folded Border:** Press the 1¼" Folded Border strips in half wrong sides together.

4. Match raw edges of Folded Border to opposite sides of top. Sew with 10 stitches per inch and a seam slightly less than ¼". Do not open out. Trim edges straight with top.

5. Sew Folded Borders on two remaining sides, and trim.

6. Sew Borders to top.

7. Layer with batting and backing. Safety pin baste.

8. Machine quilt by stitching in the ditch around the Lattice and Baskets.

9. Add binding.

Eleanor Burns

211

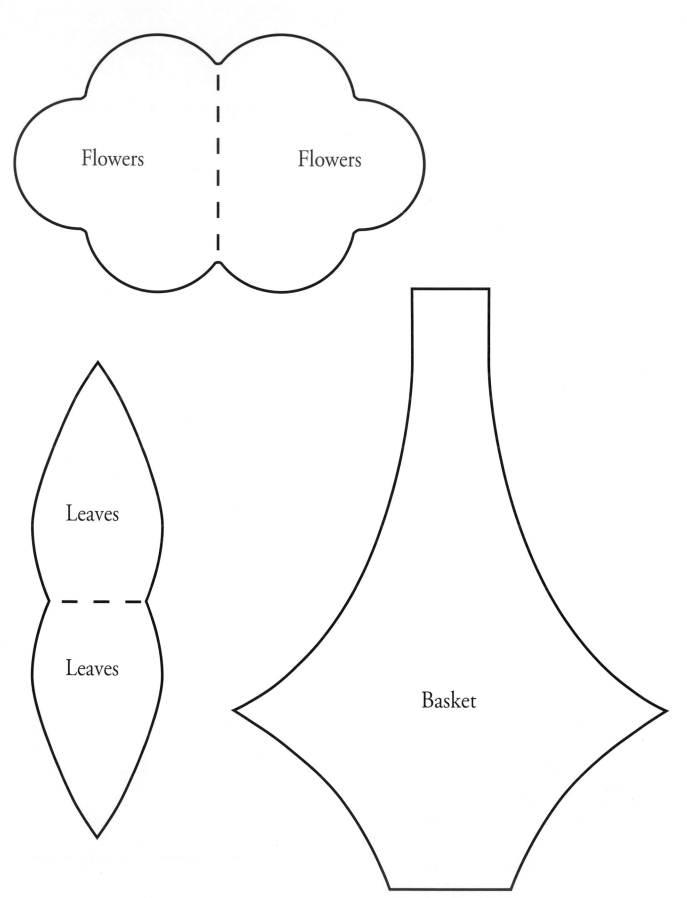

Flowers

Flowers

Leaves

Leaves

Basket

French Bouquet Wallhanging

Aiko Rogers   *Approximate Finished Size: 27" square*

Yardage

Applique Pieces

Light to Medium Weight Non-woven Fusible Interfacing
  ⅓ yd

Bow
  7" square
  1¼" x 2½" strip for center

Birds
  5" x 9" for Body
  3½" square for Wings

Green
  ¼ yd
      (3) 1¼" x 9" bias strips for Stems
      (1) 2" square for top of stem

Five Leaves
  (1) 4½" x 12"
  or make fussy cuts

Jonquil
  4½" medium yellow squares for Base A
  3" x 16" light yellow for Petal E
  2½"x 3½" dark yellow for Center

Fuchsia
  (1) 6" x 12" dark purple tops
  (6) 2½" x 3½" fuchsia bottoms

Harebell
  (2) 3½" x 7" pieces light purple
  (3) 3½" x 7" pieces medium blue
  (2) 3½" x 7" pieces dark purple

Finishing

Lt Background
  ½ yd
      (1) 16" square

Corner Triangles
  ⅜ yd
      (2) 12½" squares

Folded Border
  ¼ yd
      (4) 1¼" x 24" strips

Border
  ⅓ yd
      (2) 2½" x 24" strips
      (2) 2½" x 28" strips

Binding
  ⅓ yd
      (3) 2¾" strips

Backing
  30" square

Lightweight Batting
  30" square

Making Applique Pieces

1. Trace these pieces on fusible interfacing. Pin dotted fusible side of interfacing to right side of corresponding fabric.

   five leaves
   bow
   two bow ties
   two birds
   two wings
   top of stem
   Jonquil Base A from page 135

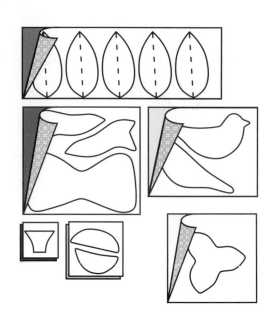

2. Sew on lines, trim, turn, and press with wooden iron.

3. Stuff bow, birds, wings, and leaves with 100% cotton batting.

Making Stems

1. Place 16" Background square on stem placement sheet. Trace three stem lines.

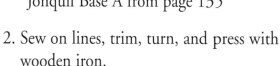

2. Place bias strips wrong side up on pressing mat. Fold up one end of each strip and press.

3. Fold in half lengthwise wrong sides together and press.

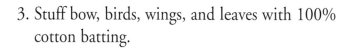

4. Starting with center stem, line up raw edge on left side of line. Stitch in place with ¼" seam.

5. Fold stem over, covering raw edges. Stitch in place. Repeat on two remaining stems.

6. Fuse top of stem in place, and stitch.

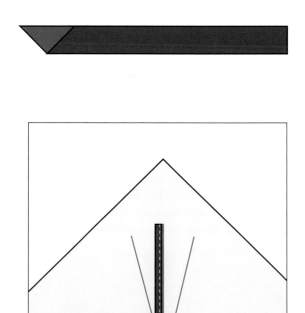

Finishing Bow

1. Press under raw edges of center strip. Tuck in bow at center, and wrap strip around center to give it dimension.

2. Tack ends of strip together in back.

3. Place Bow on top of stems. Finish outside edges.

Making Leaves

1. Triple stitch vein lines down center of each leaf.

2. Place background square on placement sheet, and arrange five leaves.

3. Fuse in place and finish outside edges.

Making Jonquil

1. Make dimensional Jonquil, following directions on pages 132–137 for Base A, Petals E, and Center.

2. Referring to placement sheet, place Base A on top of stem. Fuse in place, and finish outside edges. Finish with Petals E and Center.

Making Harebells

1. Make seven dimensional Harebells following directions on pages 78–83.

2. Arrange flowers and stitch to background with French knots.

Making Fuchsia

1. Make six tops and six dimensional bottoms following directions on pages 64–69.

2. With green pearl cotton, backstitch stems and arrange fuchsia. Finish with embroidered stamens.

Adding Corner Triangles

1. Cut two 12½" squares in half on one diagonal. If using directional fabric, cut diagonal lines in opposite directions.

2. Carefully center and pin triangles on two opposite sides. Triangles should extend equally on each end. Sew in place. Press seams toward triangles.

3. Repeat with remaining two triangles.

4. Place on gridded cutting mat and **sliver trim** to straighten outside edges. **Leave ⅝"** seam to accommodate Folded Border.

Finishing

1. Sew French knots to Birds for eyes.

2. Fuse in place, and finish outside edges.

3. Add folded border and border.

4. Machine quilt and bind.

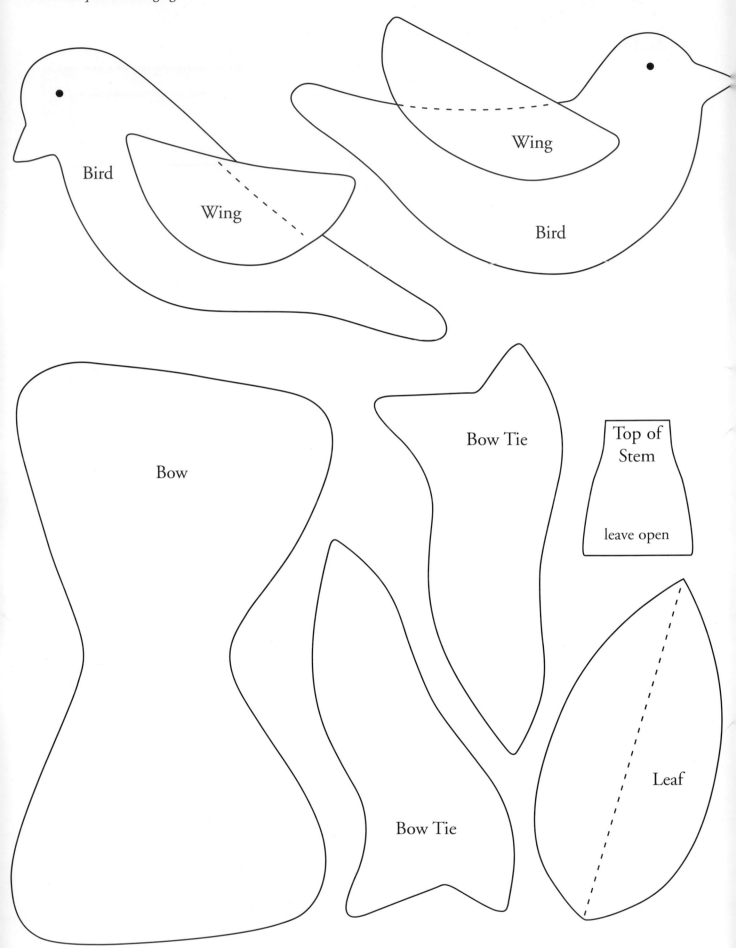

Bird

Wing

Wing

Bird

Bow

Bow Tie

Top of
Stem

leave open

Bow Tie

Leaf

Patty's Flower Pot

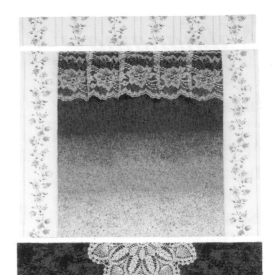

1. Center pattern and sew lace curtain along top edge of background. Lengthen stitch to 3.0 or 10 stitches per inch, and use less than ¼" seam allowance. If using flat lace, make four small pleats 3" apart.

2. Pin wall paper strips to two opposite sides of blue background. Sew ¼" seam following the edge of the stripe carefully. Press and square ends of strips.

3. **Top strip:** Pin in place along top edge lining up stripe with side strips. Stitch in place, with stitch length at 3.0. Press. Avoid hot iron on nylon lace.

4. **Window ledge:** Fold strip in half widthwise and crease center. Line up center of strip with center of doiley. Pin and sew in place, using long zig-zag stitch to prevent fraying. Center, pin and sew window ledge to bottom edge of background fabric. Lengthen stitch when sewing across doiley. Press and square corners.

5. **Making Appliques:** Make flower pot applique and stuff with cotton batting. Make three sets of pansies and two leaves, following instructions on pages 90–95.

6. **Arranging Flowers:** Center flower pot on top of doiley. Steam press in place and finish edges. Arrange three pansies and leaves to determine placement of stems. Pencil in stem lines. Remove flowers and sew stems in place. Replace flowers and turn over tops of leaves. Press in place, and finish edges. With embroidery floss or pearl cotton, embellish center of flowers.

7. Machine quilt and bind.

Index

Acknowledgements

We are grateful for all of you that help us produce accurate instructions, and beautiful finished samples. In addition, we give these friends special recognition:

Joyce Yenny for her generous gift of the original Grandmother's Garden patterns.

Sue Bouchard for her beautiful traditional quilt from solid fabrics.

Diane Knight for her stunning blue background quilt with Four Roses.

Aiko Rogers for her striking French Bouquet Wallhanging.

Jayne Bowman for creativity in designing the Basket stencil and quilting the vintage Grandmother's Garden quilt.

Teresa Varnes for being the "ghost quilter with nimble fingers" and putting in incredible hours.

Carol Ann Selepec for fantastic free-motion designs and machine quilting under strenuous deadlines.

Our Students who test our patterns, and give valuable feedback and advice.

Merritt Voigtlander, Robin Green, and Wayne Norton for turning our words and craft into a beautiful book.

The Staff at Benartex, Inc. for manufacturing the beautiful *Anniversary Florals* fabrics to compliment the Grandmother's Garden Quilt.

Mary Pat and Mike Henderson at QuiltSMART® for producing pre-printed fusible interfacing that saves us hours of time.

Order Information

Quilt in a Day books offer a wide range of techniques and are directed toward a variety of skill levels. If you do not have a quilt shop in your area, you may write or call for a complete catalog and current price list of all books and patterns published by Quilt in a Day®, Inc.

Quilt in a Day®, Inc. 1955 Diamond Street, San Marcos, CA 92069
www.quilt-in-a-day.com
Toll Free: 1 800 777-4852 Fax: (760) 591-4424
8 am to 5 pm Pacific Time

Anniversary Florals

by Eleanor Burns

Style #242 Flower Basket

Color A
Rose

Color B
Blue

Color C
Light Blue

Color D
Dark Purple

Color F
Lilac

Color G
Light Beige

Color H
Light Rose

Style #244 Lilacs

Color A
Pink

Color B
Blue

Color C
Peach

Color D
Lilac

Style #247 Floral Vine

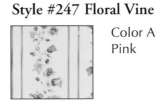
Color A
Pink

Color B
Blue

Color C
Yellow

Color D
Lilac

Style #245 Narcissus

Color A
Pink

Color B
Blue

Color C
Peach

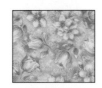
Color D
Lilac

Color E
Beige

Style #242 Springtime

Color A
Pink & Pink

Color B
Pink & Blue

Color C
Blue & Yellow

Color D
Lilac & Beige

Style #246 Flower Puffs

Color A
Pink & Blue

Color B
Blue

Color C
Yellow & Peach

Color D
Lilac

Style #243 Forget-Me-Nots

Color A
Rose

Color B
Blue

Color C
Yellow & Blue

Color D
Purple

Style #248 Eleanor's Ombre´

Color B
Blue

Color E
Natural

Color D
Olive

Color F
Green

Style #241 Eleanor's Lace

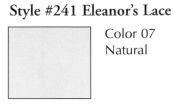
Color 07
Natural

Ask for these fabrics by name at your local quilt shop